Advance Praise for
ON EQUAL TERMS
Redefining China's Relationship with America and the West

With the emergence of China as an important economic power, readers will benefit immensely from Zheng Mingxun's views and observations given his distinctive vantage point as an accomplished leader in both China and the U.S. In this important book, he sets out to foster greater objectivity and understanding between China and the West. Management at multinational corporations interested in China will benefit from his rich and balanced insights on this often challenging and increasingly complex market.

Tom Neff
Chairman
Spencer Stuart USA

China has risen to become the second largest economy in the world. Nevertheless, it is still a developing and emerging nation. The U.S. is the most developed country and the world's leading superpower. No bilateral relationship today would be more crucial in shaping the global order and agenda than the one between China and the U.S. in the twenty-first century. Zheng Mingxun with his bi-cultural background has written this thoughtful book to help readers in the West better understand the complexities and intricacies of China. Hopefully, leaders in both the private and public sectors, not only in America but also in the West as a whole will heed his observations and advice.

C H Tung
Vice Chairman of Chinese People's
Political Consultative Conference
Former Chief Executive of Hong Kong

China's rise is changing the global equation. Zheng Mingxun with his East-West background has written this timely book to encourage readers in the West to have a more objective and balanced view on China. Reading *On Equal Terms* will be a good starting point for practitioners in both the private and public sectors to better appreciate the cultural and ideological differences between China and the West.

Francesco Trapani
Chief Executive Officer
Bulgari Group

ON EQUAL TERMS

*Redefining China's Relationship
with America and the West*

ON EQUAL TERMS

---

*Redefining China's Relationship
with America and the West*

Zheng Mingxun

WILEY

John Wiley & Sons (Asia) Pte. Ltd.

Other Wiley Editorial Offices
John Wiley & Sons, 111 River Street, Hoboken, NJ 07030, USA
John Wiley & Sons, The Atrium, Southern Gate, Chichester, West Sussex, P019 8SQ,
    United Kingdom
John Wiley & Sons (Canada) Ltd., 5353 Dundas Street West, Suite 400, Toronto,
    Ontario, M9B 6HB, Canada
John Wiley & Sons Australia Ltd., 42 McDougall Street, Milton, Queensland 4064,
    Australia
Wiley-VCH, Boschstrasse 12, D-69469 Weinheim, Germany

Library of Congress Cataloging-in-Publication Data
ISBN 978-0-470-82886-1 (Hardcover)
ISBN 978-0-470-82888-5 (ePDF)
ISBN 978-0-470-82887-8 (Mobi)
ISBN 978-0-470-82889-2 (ePub)

Typeset in 11/14 Sabon Roman by MPS Limited, a Macmillan Company
Printed in Singapore by Markon Print Media Pte. Ltd.

10 9 8 7 6 5 4 3 2 1

For my wife, Janet, for her untiring support and extraordinary patience during the many hours I spent on this project.

For my international bunch of children and grandchildren spread across the world—be happy and live your lives to the fullest.

CONTENTS

Foreword   ix

Acknowledgments   xi

Introduction: An East-West Journey   1

1 The Hybrid Machine   17
   Governance with Chinese characteristics

2 Guns and Roses   31
   Expect a roller-coaster ride

3 The Chinese Piggy Bank   45
   The global shift in economic relations

4 Not Made in China   61
   Why the U.S. trade deficit with
   China is not what it seems

5 Land of Many Markets   71
   "The mountains are high and the emperor is far away"

6 *Guanxi* and *Mianzi*   87
   Still important despite legal reform

7 Soft Power   97
   Winning hearts and minds

8 Climbing the Technology Ladder   115
   From "Assembled in China" to "Innovated in China"

9 Winds of Change   133
   China's drive for alternative energy is gaining
   worldwide attention and respect

10 The Dream Team   145
    China and America must put politics aside and work
    together for the benefit of the planet and for future
    generations

Afterword   159

Appendix A: China's Current Leadership   163

Appendix B: China-U.S. Joint Statement   165

Glossary   179

Notes   185

Index   191

FOREWORD

For many Americans, the middle two weeks of August 2008 were spent glued to the television, watching the athletes of the world compete in the Summer Olympic Games in Beijing—China's first turn as host nation. More countries than ever before took home at least one medal from the competition, with Chinese athletes winning the most gold medals and American athletes winning the most medals overall. Yet for many viewers, the event was as much an eye-opening introduction to the new China as it was an entertaining international competition. Who can forget the magnificent opening ceremony, which was kicked off by 2,008 perfectly synchronized drummers and told the story of five thousand years of Chinese history?

Certainly China wanted us to be impressed. The 2008 Olympics were a major statement of economic status and a unique vehicle for communicating the China brand to the rest of the world. China is now the second-largest economy in the world, behind the United States, and the fastest-growing G20 economy. It is also the largest trading nation—the largest exporter of commodities and the second-largest importer after the United States. This ancient nation has without a doubt arrived on the modern economic stage.

But what, many Westerners rightly ask, does this mean for us? There is a temptation to think in terms of competition, with China's rise somehow foreshadowing the future decline of the United States. This is somewhat paranoid—and it is the wrong way to conceive of our relationship. We cannot say for sure what the world will look like in twenty, thirty, or forty years, but we do know that the United States and China are the major powers right now, and with power comes responsibility. If we have learned anything from the Cold War, it is that cooperation and collaboration are the way forward, and such progress is possible only when both powers exercise mutual respect and understanding. Simply put, Americans need to know more about China—its unique history, values, and systems—so that we can work together for the greater good.

So argues Zheng Mingxun—or Paul Cheng, as I know him—in his book, *On Equal Terms*. Straddling our two countries with clear eyes and profound knowledge, Paul understands, and has sympathy for, both China and the United States. But he also has many suggestions for both countries. He offers them quietly and in a gentle way, with conviction based on a unique perspective that few others will ever have. Born in China, educated in the United States, having worked for multinationals and having served in both the public and private sectors in his home country, Paul is more than a national treasure—he is a global treasure.

For an American, I am a relatively experienced China hand. Over the years I have taught in several Chinese executive education programs, and I currently sit on the boards of several prominent Chinese business schools. But even I was surprised, riveted, and enlightened to read Paul's book and find that, in aggregate, I knew so little about China and the ways it has both changed and remained the same over the decades. As a Western-trained Chinese business leader watching his country's transition to a market economy, Paul brings us an indispensable perspective.

As he tells us here, the Chinese term for *business*, *sheng yi*, can also translate into English as "create new meanings." This is what the United States and China must do going forward, and it is what Paul himself has done in this fine book. He implores Americans to reconsider China, to try to understand this rising power on its own terms and not merely through a Western lens. The results of such understanding—and a mutual effort on the part of Chinese—will be of great benefit to Americans and Chinese alike, and indeed, to the entire world.

Thomas S. Robertson
Dean of the Wharton School
University of Pennsylvania

ACKNOWLEDGMENTS

I would like to thank my mother, Madame Tan Jen-Chiu, who brought me up single-handedly and who instilled in me one of her favorite prayers:

> O Lord, thank thee for the friends who need me, to give me a purpose in Life
> Thank thee for those whom I need to teach me the meaning of humility
> Thank thee, Lord, for the friends who have wronged me for how else do I learn to forgive?

I was fortunate to have met Don Sedgwick, chairman and part-owner of the Transatlantic Literary Agency, who was my agent for this project. I am grateful for his invaluable support and encouragement. David Hayes, the Canadian feature writer, assisted me with editing my draft to ensure the book will be an easy read for general readers. He along with a Chinese student in Toronto, Zhang Cuiping, also contributed valuable research.

I want to thank Nick Melchior, senior editor at John Wiley & Sons (Asia), together with his team of Joel Balbin, Karin Seet and Cindy Chu for their advice and support and for their confidence in me as a first-time author.

Last but not least, I would also like to thank Hilary Powers for her diligence with the copy-editing process and Professor Guo Rongxing, author of *How the Chinese Economy Works*, who acted as independent reader and reviewer for Wiley, for his valuable suggestions and advice.

Otherwise, as I said in the Introduction, this is one man's "home cooking." I hope you will enjoy it.

INTRODUCTION

AN EAST-WEST JOURNEY

My life has been an interesting East-West journey. I am Chinese, but I spent more than a decade in America attending college, completing graduate business school, and working in New York City. Then I returned to my home—Hong Kong. During that journey, I had a front-row seat for two of the world's top news events of the past half-century. I watched the rise of China as a potential global force, and I followed its complicated and changing relationship with the West, particularly the United States. As I viewed all these events, I was reminded of an old Chinese proverb: *Those who play the game do not see it as clearly as those who watch.*

Today we are amazed at China's dramatic changes—a shift in influence and power, becoming the second-largest economy and the largest exporter in the world. More automobiles are sold each day in China than in the United States. This is remarkable because there were only a few private cars in China just fifteen years ago. On October 1, 2010, China moved closer to its goal of landing on the moon as the Chang'e-2 satellite was successfully launched. This probe plans to test technology in preparation for an unmanned moon landing in 2013.

The phenomenon of new wealth in China now exists in eastern coastal cities such as Shanghai, Beijing, and Guangzhou, with some exceptional cases in selected second-tier cities. *Forbes*'s latest list of the world's richest billionaires ranked China (including Hong Kong) with 119 (some sources are even quoting a figure of 150), second only to the United States.[1] And wealthy Chinese are not just buying property and luxury products (cars, watches, jewelry). With forty more airports planned across the country, tens of millions of dollars are being spent on private jets (Gulfstream, Cessna, and Bell Helicopter all regard China as their next big market opportunity). We are seeing a form of keeping-up-with-the-Joneses mentality (or should I say keeping-up-with-the-Wangs?) that no one associated with China a mere generation ago. Early in 2011, *China Daily* reported that a Chinese buyer paid 156,000 euros ($208,000) for a racing pigeon at an auction in Belgium, setting a new world record—a signal that the sport is taking off in China. The bird, named Blue Prince, has a pedigree full of Belgian champions—considered to be the best in the racing-pigeon world. At another auction, a 218-bird collection was apparently snapped up by Chinese buyers for 1.37 million euros ($1.82 million).[2]

Hardly a day passes without a story about China in the pages of the *Financial Times*, *Wall Street Journal*, or *International Herald Tribune* echoing statements made by Paul JJ Payack, president of the Global Language Monitor. His publication boldly reported in 2009 that the rise of China was by far the most widely read story of the past decade—and that period included 9/11, the war in Iraq and Afghanistan, and the global financial crisis. "The rise of China to new economic heights has changed—and continues to challenge—the current international order," Payack proclaimed. "It is with little surprise that its ongoing transformation has topped all news stories in a decade bespotted by war, economic catastrophe, and natural disasters."[3]

I get to view these changes from Hong Kong, which is an extraordinary hybrid of East and West. In fact, CNN recently suggested fifty reasons why Hong Kong is the number one "world city."[4] Cosmopolitan and vibrant, it is where Chinese and many other nationalities congregate. For decades it has been a gateway to China, as well as the Asia-Pacific regional headquarters for many multinationals. A large number of mainland Chinese companies today raise capital for expansion on the Hong Kong Stock Exchange. And the bulk of the factories across the border, which produce a large portion of China's consumer-goods exports to the United States and Europe, are owned or managed by people from Hong Kong. In fact, Hong Kong is the ultimate middleman for trade in Asia. Hong Kong's business influence across China is extensive and deep. Thousands of overseas companies involved in China trade have established their beachheads in Hong Kong because of the city's strategic location and international business environment. Hong Kong provides capital, management skills, market knowledge, mature business infrastructure, and access to international markets. To minimize their business risk, international firms tend to place their highest-value activities in Hong Kong, including international corporate, management, procurement, distribution, finance, information, and professional services.

Many of my friends here are bi-cultural, having attended university in either America or England. We are part of China's "Shift Generation," helping to build a bridge between China and the West. It is our deepest wish that China and the West, especially America, maintain an interdependent relationship—one built on mutual trust. The well-being of the rest of the world depends on this delicate relationship.

Countless articles and books have been written in recent years about China's rise in international stature. However, mass media in the West sometimes focus on negative or sensational events and make judgments based on a Western point of view, so it is easy for the public and politicians in the West to fall prey to a particular slant on the news. This kind of coverage, in my opinion, does little to promote better understanding between the two cultures. Similarly, there are influential scholars and intellectuals in the West who believe that every country in the world should adopt a democratic political system, regardless of that nation's history. Even some Chinese refugees who fled to the West from the communist uprising have written articles and books with a similarly one-sided view about developments since Mao Zedong proclaimed the formation of the People's Republic of China.

When misunderstandings and myths are repeated frequently, especially by those who appear to be in authority, they often become accepted truths. For instance, in 2010 the United States was putting considerable pressure on China to revalue its currency, variously referred to as the Renminbi (RMB) or yuan. (For simplicity's sake, I will speak of yuan hereafter.) As enlightened economists tell us, a country's currency is only considered undervalued if the combined trade in goods and services, as compared to the rest of the world, is always showing a surplus. A bilateral surplus (as in the case of China and the United States) does not necessarily mean a currency is undervalued. China may still have a zero, or even a negative, trade balance compared to the rest of the world.

Most non–oil-producing countries have chronic trade deficits when compared to oil-producing countries. Perhaps the counterargument in the case of China and America is that the U.S. dollar is overvalued. In any event, by early summer of 2010 the Chinese government, which holds a considerable amount of U.S. treasuries, had allowed the yuan to rise more than 20 percent since 2005, and it will probably continue to make adjustments, albeit on a carefully managed and gradual basis.

One other myth is that China's exports represent a significant portion of its GDP. In layman's terms, China is only assembling products from raw materials that are brought into the country and then sent back—sometimes to the same country. Therefore, the portion of the value of a particular product that remains in China is actually quite small. The importance of these exports, in fact, is more related to job creation for China's large workforce and the necessity of feeding a population of 1.3 billion people.

These and other misconceptions could be alleviated with more objective reporting and less political speculation. It is fair to say that most people in the West have neither visited nor lived in China. If we are going to build some communication bridges, reporters will have to temper their analysis with more knowledge of the culture, customs, and values of China, and the challenges it still faces. This is an enormous country trying to sustain economic growth to maintain social stability.

Cooperation rather than criticism is one of the underpinnings of this book. It is critical for the sake of future generations that America and China provide joint leadership to help solve pressing issues facing the world, including poverty, disease, terrorism, and climate change—rather than remaining preoccupied with geopolitics and national interests. I believe that the United States and China, in their respective ways, are both great nations, and there is no need for relations between them to be a train wreck of colliding cultures. And this brings me to the principal reason I have written this book.

On Equal Terms is neither a traditional memoir nor an autobiography. Having worked for major American multinationals in both the United States and Asia, and been involved in politics in Hong Kong, I have lived with a foot in both worlds. My motivation is to try to help people in the West better understand China. China is not a military threat. It is a tough economic competitor, yes, but Americans are born competitors as well—from sports to the national habit of ranking almost everything. Mutual respect is the key to any relationship. It is the gate that opens to the path we must take if we ever hope to achieve world peace.

My goal is to provide insights on selected issues relating to business, politics, and culture as they unfold today and have unfolded in the recent past. Through this lens I hope to suggest what the public in the West might understand about some Chinese actions, and what China's rise will ultimately mean to the world. This is a personal narrative and not a textbook. There will be minimal references to numbers and charts, because I prefer simply to share my observations and personal experience with you. As someone who likes good food but has no pretension of being a great chef, I would like you to think of *On Equal Terms* as an invitation into my kitchen. The book is one man's home cooking rather than anything resembling nouvelle cuisine.

The challenge for me is to remain as neutral and objective as possible because I respect and love both China and America and the many values represented by the West. But because I am trying to explain China's positions from a Chinese perspective, I hope you will take this into consideration and not feel I am overly defending my country. China is just beginning to embark on a long and winding road to becoming a responsible member of the global society.

My Journey So Far

I was born in 1936 on a small island called Gulangyu off the southeastern coast of China (across from Taiwan). It is a five-minute ferry ride from the bigger island city of Xiamen (formerly Amoy), which is now one of the country's economic powerhouses. Many Taiwanese investments are located here. Since the signing of the trade pact between China and Taiwan, Xiamen has taken on added importance due to its close proximity. For example, the four-teenth China International Fair for Investment and Trade and Development was held here in September 2010. As reported by the *China Daily*, U.S. Undersecretary of State Robert Hormats lauded Chinese Vice President Xi Jinping's opening speech illus-trating China's move to optimize its investment climate as "very constructive."[5]

Gulangyu has a fascinating history. It was designated a spe-cial zone for consulates, missionaries, and foreign traders after the Treaty of Nanking in 1842, which accounts for its famous European-style architecture. Today some of these beautiful build-ings have been restored, but others are in need of major renovation. Gulangyu is also known as "Piano Island" because foreign-run schools emphasized piano lessons for children. Today there are an estimated 200 pianos in homes around the island. Aside from electric golf carts for tourists, no motor vehicles are allowed.

My grandparents' house remains on a hill in a quiet part of the island, with a commanding view of the strait separating the island from Xiamen. There are still family pictures and some original furniture in the building, although the house is unoccupied. All my relatives are now living in Xiamen, a much larger city across the strait from Gulangyu. But there is at least one thing that has not changed in the house. An old piano still stands in a corner of one of the rooms.

My grandfather, the first ethnic Chinese headmaster of the island's Anglo-Chinese school, loved to cook, so he used to make his own soy sauce in the backyard. After Japan invaded China in 1937, he fled with his entire family to Hong Kong. Together with a friend, he founded Amoy Canning Corporation, which became a successful food company known for its Gold Label soy sauce.

My father, the number three son (in those days families tended to have many children, who were often referred to by number in order of birth), studied sociology at Yenching University in Beijing (today it is part of Peking University) before attending graduate school at the University of Washington in Seattle shortly before the outbreak of World War II. My mother and I were to join him, but by then Hong Kong was under Japanese occupation and we stayed to look after my grandparents.

During the war I watched American planes coming off aircraft carriers in the South China Sea to bomb the territory every few days. Whenever an oil depot was hit, the sky would turn orange for hours—sometimes for days. Hong Kong residents were caught in the middle of this struggle. Often our daily diet was just a ball of rice with some soy sauce. As a child I witnessed barbaric behavior on the part of the Japanese military, which I try not to recall too often. Today I have many Japanese friends who, like me, are part of a generation too young to have been involved with the atrocities. Together we are focused on peace and prosperity for both our nations.

After the war, my mother took me to Tianjin, a port city located 130 kilometers (80 miles) southeast of Beijing, where her family lived. I briefly attended elementary school and had my grounding in Mandarin (the language referred to as *Putonghua* in pinyin) before returning to Hong Kong to attend high school. My father eventually became a professor of sociology at the University of Hawaii and remarried. Meanwhile, my mother devoted her life to the YWCA movement, first as a staff member and later as president of the Hong Kong YWCA. At that time she became friends with Lilace Reid Barnes, an American philanthropist and social reformer who was head of the World YWCA from 1947 to 1955. When my mother mentioned that she planned to send her only son to university in the United States, Lilace Barnes suggested Lake Forest College, a small liberal arts institution north of Chicago. (The Barnes mansion was across the road from the campus, and her family were major donors to the college.)

The advice was well received. I accepted a scholarship at Lake Forest, where I majored in biology and chemistry. Anxious to be part of college life, I joined a fraternity (Tau Kappa Epsilon), played varsity tennis, became active in extracurricular activities, and was elected president of the fraternity in my senior year. In the summers, I worked as a counselor at a YMCA canoe-tripping camp in northern Wisconsin. At the time, I was one of very few foreign students and, unlike many exchange students today, I could not afford to return to Hong Kong for holidays. Instead, I was invited by classmates to their family homes over Thanksgiving, Christmas, and Easter holidays. As a result, I became familiar with American culture, values, and lifestyles.

My mother had hoped I would become a doctor, but my aptitude test scores were not quite high enough to get into a medical school. Instead, I received a grant to do a year of neurophysiological research at the University of Oregon. This was around the time that Phil Knight and Bill Bowerman, his athletic coach at the university, started Blue Ribbon Sports, the company that eventually evolved into the global powerhouse of Nike Inc. (It has been reported that the two founders consummated their agreement on a handshake, more like an Asian practice than the complex contracts of the highly legalistic North American business world.)

Undertaking that research project helped me realize I was not cut out for the medical world (the aptitude test was right). Instead, I decided that my true calling would be in the field of business. I was accepted into the Wharton graduate program at the University of Pennsylvania and in 1961 I completed my MBA. My first job was as a systems engineer trainee with IBM. The company had just introduced the 1400 series, the second generation of midrange computers for business. But not being technically inclined, I decided to shift my career into consumer marketing. I joined the Vick Chemical Company, known for its cough and cold products. (It would soon be renamed Richardson-Merrell and, later still, be acquired by Procter & Gamble.) I was initially in market research before moving into brand management.

In the mid-sixties, I persuaded the company to send me back to Asia, where I felt I could make the greatest contribution. I was first based in Singapore as market manager for Singapore and later in Malaysia. In late 1967, I was given a promotion at Vick Chemical and asked to manage the Southeast Asia region from Bangkok. Two years later, I was recruited by the Warner-Lambert Company, maker of brands such as Listerine, Schick, Trident, and Dentyne, and assigned to its office in Hong Kong as marketing manager for Asia. I was thrilled to be home after more than a decade away. In the early seventies, I visited Taiwan regularly as we were building a factory there. When I became chairman of the Hong Kong General Chamber of Commerce in the nineties, I also chaired the (then named) Hong Kong–Taipei Business Cooperative Committee.

In 1976, the executive search giant Spencer Stuart & Associates tried to recruit me on behalf of one of its clients. Instead, I ended up joining Spencer Stuart to launch its Asian practice. Two years later I was elected a global partner of the firm and eventually I opened offices in Tokyo and Singapore, in addition to Hong Kong. At that time, headhunting was not as well known a profession as it is today, but I discovered that helping corporations identify the right management team was a satisfying experience. Through this work I met many executives in the region, both as clients and as candidates. Today, many of them have become leaders in their industries.

In 1987, I was invited to join Inchcape Pacific, one of the long-standing British trading companies—referred to by the Chinese as *hongs*—as an executive director. The company was a conglomerate involved in a wide range of businesses: car dealerships, insurance brokering, and shipping, and it acted as distributor for many consumer and industrial products. It employed thousands of people across the region. (James Clavell's best-selling novel *Tai-Pan* was based on one of these *hongs*.) I became chairman in 1992 and, a few years later, I was also asked by Sir Evelyn de Rothschild to become non-executive chairman of the N. M. Rothschild & Sons Hong Kong operation.

In Hong Kong at that time there were no elections, nor was there a democratic system. The territory thrived as an entrepôt and as the gateway to China, driven by Chinese business entrepreneurs who created most of the jobs. Under British colonial rule, legislators were appointed by the governor, who in turn was appointed by the queen of England on recommendation of the British prime minster. Governor Sir David Wilson appointed me to the Legislative Council in 1988, and I served during those tumultuous years leading up to Britain's handover of Hong Kong back to China in 1997. Looking back, I am glad to have been involved in this historic change.

In the early nineties, with this big event approaching, Britain decided to inject democracy into the colony by initiating a partial process of political elections. As a result, half of today's seats in the Hong Kong legislature are through direct election, which many viewed at the time as a double standard. China was not very happy with this development, so the leaders decided to form a preparatory committee composed of indigenous Hong Kong business and community leaders and the number-two ranking members of the key ministries in Beijing.

At this time, I was chairman of the Hong Kong General Chamber of Commerce, so I was asked to join this committee. We went to Beijing monthly for meetings to plan every facet of the handover, from the political system to education, health care, and social welfare. During those years, I had the opportunity to meet and work with the highest-ranking leaders, such as Jiang Zemin, Li Peng, Zhu Rongji, Qiao Shi, and Lu Ping. It was apparent that China valued Hong Kong as a crown jewel and would do everything possible to ensure that it continued to thrive as a cosmopolitan city, albeit one designated a Special Administrative Region of China. Deng Xiaoping, who was head of the Communist Party and the reformer who led China toward a "socialist market economy," developed his "One Country, Two Systems" concept for Hong Kong during this period. (He also planned to apply this principle to Macao and, hopefully, one day to Taiwan.) When *Fortune* magazine published an article titled "The Death of Hong Kong," it showed just how wrong the international media occasionally can be when analyzing Eastern politics.

In 1999, after serving on the provisional legislature for one year, I read a book that literally changed my life: *Repacking Your Bags: Lighten Your Load for the Rest of Your Life*.[6] This international bestseller (written by two Americans, Richard Leider and David Shapiro) explained that we can only truly enjoy our lives if we enjoy our work, are content with our personal relationships, and live where we truly want to live. Such simple and obvious advice. It dawned on me I was so busy that I did not have a life of my own. As a result, I decided not to seek reelection, and to retire from corporate life so I could have more time to myself and for my family.

Of course, I would not have been happy to stop working entirely. I now prefer to say I am a "free man," rather than someone who has retired. For the past ten years I have been involved with private equity activities, and I sit on boards as an independent, non-executive director. I also advise multinationals on their operations in Asia. I am, for example, deputy chairman and an independent director of Esprit Holdings, a prominent fashion company that has annual revenues of US$4 billion. I also launched a private equity fund named the China High Growth Fund with two partners in January 2011.

In 2005, the Hong Kong government approached me to chair a privatization project. Over the years, the government had developed low-income housing throughout the territory to meet demand from the influx of Chinese migrants. Each of the more than one hundred locations had a shopping arcade with car parking facilities. The government thought the private sector could do a better job of managing these arcades, so it privatized them into a Real Estate Investment Trust (REIT) that it listed on the Hong Kong Stock Exchange. Raising approximately US$2.5 billion, it was the world's largest REIT initial public offering at that time. As chairman of Link Management, I was responsible for managing this portfolio of shopping arcades and car parks.

Unfortunately, an international hedge fund bought more than 18 percent of the shares shortly after the listing and together with other hedge funds began to impose a new agenda, ignoring the fact that these arcades were designed to serve low-income housing residents. As arcades were renovated and leases came up for renewal, these investors pressured the board and management to kick out small tenants in favor of large chain stores to obtain higher rents, which was contrary to the original vision. I resigned in protest in 2007 and subsequently wrote a case for the Hong Kong University of Science and Technology's business school— to remind and encourage future leaders that business is not just about making a profit, and that social responsibility is also important.

Another development worth mentioning is my involvement with the Honolulu-based East-West Center, for which I am co-chair of the Foundation Board. The East-West Center is a non-profit education and research organization conceived in the late 1950s by Senator Lyndon B. Johnson. In 1960, President

Dwight Eisenhower signed the act that created it, and a year later President John F. Kennedy, another supporter, authorized even greater federal funding for it. The center's goal, which I share, is to promote stronger relations and better understanding between the United States and Asia.

I still travel regularly into mainland China, both on leisure and on business. China's transformation continues to amaze me, although the leaders in Beijing will face a mountain of challenges to sustain the country's economic momentum in the coming years while still maintaining social stability. China continues to follow one of Deng Xiaoping's often-quoted sayings, "Crossing the river by feeling for the stones." Steadily, through trial and error and lessons absorbed from the West, the country has become a more active member in the international community, especially since joining the World Trade Organization in 2001. With the shifting fortunes of the developed West and power moving to emerging markets, the G20 (in which China was a founding member), rather than the G8, is becoming the relevant forum for international dialogue.

I see these changes during my frequent visits to America. There I observe a society that is increasingly inner-directed, partly as a result of domestic politics. With unemployment at an all-time high, some segments of society are understandably disillusioned. Local news often features crimes involving guns (the Arizona tragedy in January is a sad example), while the preoccupation with sex scandals would seem to indicate a society in some turmoil. Yet I have no doubt that America will keep innovating as it transforms itself further as a high-technology powerhouse. Its so-called soft power (entertainment, sports, fashion) will continue to be an enormous cultural and business influence around the world, while its military supremacy will ensure that its superpower status remains intact for years to come. (All you have to do is attend an NFL or college football game to witness the fighting spirit of Americans.)

But the world is changing. At one time, the Soviet Union was America's counterpart and rival in the East, and the prevailing Cold War attitude was confrontational: "friend or foe." Today, the new rising power is China. And although the attitude is less overtly confrontational, citizens in the West, particularly in the

United States, need to know more about China. In fact, even what they think they know may be fueled by misconceptions and misunderstandings. My interest in writing *On Equal Terms* grew in large part from my belief that misunderstandings are counterproductive—in world affairs as well as business. We need to shift our focus and shift our perceptions.

Looking Ahead

America and China have the potential to join forces and help make the world a better place—but only if the eagle and the phoenix can share the same nest. Let me explain this avian metaphor, which has many symbolic and historical roots in both countries.

America is accustomed to being a world superpower, dominant in everything from business and culture to military strength. But I wonder about its broader perspective on international affairs. I am not convinced that Americans are always aware of the cultural and societal values of geographically distant countries. Although various statistics are offered for the number of Americans with passports, the U.S. State Department suggests the accurate figure is 68 million. Stated differently, only one out of every five people in the United States has a passport and is therefore likely to have gone outside the country's borders. In my own experience, traveling abroad has been an essential part of my education—particularly with regard to the two current superpowers.

An eagle is depicted on the Great Seal of the United States holding a bundle of thirteen arrows in its left talon (symbolizing the original thirteen states) and an olive branch in its right. In combination this illustrates that the nation has "a strong desire for peace but will always be ready for war." (Although the eagle's head is turned toward the olive branch, suggesting an emphasis on peace.)

An important part of Chinese mythology for at least seven thousand years, the phoenix is a symbol of virtue, grace, power, and prosperity. Together, the phoenix and the dragon symbolize the union of yin and yang—complementary opposites within a greater whole. According to a feng shui master, Lam Kam Chuen, "The phoenix is a mythical bird that never dies. It flies far ahead to the front always scanning the landscape and distant space. It represents our capacity for vision, for collecting sensory information about our environment and the events unfolding within it."[7] For China, a country that was often invaded—by the Mongols, the Huns, the Japanese—and a nation that built the Great Wall to protect itself, the idea of this far-seeing bird rising from the ashes to fly again is a powerful image.

The differences between the two nations can be profound. In America, there is only one language, albeit with many variations in accent from region to region. Still, a person with a Texan accent can understand a fellow American from the Bronx. And forthrightness is highly valued. The person who takes control of a situation and speaks with confidence is respected. Individual rights are entrenched in a way that citizens of a nation like China, accustomed to a "total control" style of governing, find incomprehensible. America has also evolved over the years to be an ultimate entitlement society.

China has hundreds of distinct dialects, with a sharp distinction between spoken and written language. Although most literate people can understand the written form, speakers of different dialects might as well be speaking entirely different languages. This fact, and the emphasis on formality and avoiding confrontation in China, leads to many misunderstandings. The Chinese avoid saying no, for example, because such blunt responses are considered impolite. Westerners are puzzled or even annoyed by the Chinese propensity to use indirect "soft nos," seen as a way for both parties to save face.

In *On Equal Terms*, I address these and many other complexities and misunderstandings, from culture and etiquette to financial and trade issues, from the myth of "Made in China" (most products are assembled with imported materials and parts) to the country's surprising advances in alternative energy sources (China is more green, for example, than most people realize). I talk about Western soft power—the pervasive influence of music, fast food, Hollywood entertainment, and other cultural products and the significance they have on relations. And I try to demonstrate how America's expansionist attitudes can clash with China's sensitivities based on its history of being threatened, bullied, invaded, and humiliated.

Through all the chapters, I want to build understanding that, in their hearts, the Chinese today want to focus on independence, economic development, unification, harmony, and peace. The next generation will likely see the Western-dominated unipolar system being replaced by a multipolar world. In essence, we are looking at an unprecedented modern shift in economic power from the West to the East. Although this shift will be challenging, I hope the West would welcome such a development and treat China as an international partner.

I have written *On Equal Terms* to offer a foundation for greater understanding between China and the West. I also want the book to encourage mutual trust and respect among peoples and nations, and to help us cooperate on many global challenges. In the end, the equation is not complicated, and it is very hopeful. Together, those in the East and the West have a chance to join in an epic journey to make the world a better place.

On Chinese Spellings

For readers not familiar with Chinese names and terms, please note that since 1979, China has used the pinyin method to transliterate Chinese characters into the Roman alphabet.

In most cases, I have employed pinyin spellings in this book, including my own name. For example, my name in Cantonese (the prevailing dialect used in Hong Kong) is Cheng Mingfun, whereas in pinyin (the Putonghua national dialect), it is Zheng Mingxun.

I

THE HYBRID MACHINE

GOVERNANCE WITH CHINESE CHARACTERISTICS

I still remember how excited I was when World War II ended and the GIs handed out chocolate bars as part of the celebration. In the eyes of small children, the American soldiers were larger-than-life heroes. They were the freedom fighters. So it is not surprising that I chose to spend part of my formative years in America attending college and graduate school during the fifties and early sixties. Even today many families continue to send their children to America for higher education.

As a nation, having triumphed in World War II, America was beaming with confidence. Several of my fraternity brothers were living off the GI Bill. In the decade following the war, the most popular entertainment was cowboys-and-Indians movies starring John Wayne, Gary Cooper, and Alan Ladd—heroes in white hats carrying America into a shining future. By the sixties, a revolution in pop music formed a soundtrack for a generation inspired by John F. Kennedy's charismatic leadership: "Ask not what your country can do for you—ask what you can do for your country." I was witnessing a nation evolving into a civil society based on freedom of speech, gender and racial equality, individual rights, and a democratic political system. Along with similar changes happening in Europe, this seemed to represent the modern evolution of Western civilization. But perhaps we were mistaken.

Americans I have met over the years—both socially and through business—have generally been friendly, outgoing, and well-intentioned people. Yet the postwar generation, and those that followed it, grew up not knowing hardship—only an increasingly materialistic lifestyle based on easy credit. Most people bought houses, big cars, and appliances on credit. *Enjoy now and pay later* was the common attitude. It became a land of entitlement. Americans—known as "those rich people"—were the envy of most other nations around the world. As America became a global superpower, it began to dictate norms and standards for the world to follow. Double standards inevitably surfaced, because national and corporate interests were at stake. Free-market democracy became the only viable model for all nations to adopt, regardless of their stage of history and development.

Partly as a result of the Cold War between America and Russia (which was more about nuclear balance than economics), leaders in Washington during the late seventies and early eighties decided to support China's economic reforms under the leadership of Deng Xiaoping after Mao's death in 1976. America was intent on keeping China from falling further under Russia's Communist influence, while China welcomed America as an ally that would lessen its dependence on Russia. This, in my view, was an important turning point; it led to increased globalization and today's interdependency between China and America.

Opening up the U.S. market to Chinese exports helped kickstart the miraculous growth China enjoys today. It's useful to remember that China was emerging from decades of humiliation from foreign invasion and occupation. Several generations of Chinese lived through extreme hardship and poverty under failed socialism. This was a period with an abundance of cheap labor and strong encouragement from Deng's pragmatic leadership. ("It doesn't matter if a cat is white or black; it's a good one so long as it catches mice." Or his other famous line: "To get rich is glorious.") Local factories, as well as those owned by multinationals but employing local labor, began assembling goods to satisfy a voracious hunger on the part of Americans and Europeans for almost every kind of consumer product.

It is interesting to note a distinct difference between the two systems that exists to this day. The premise behind the Western form of democracy sounds good because citizens have the power to vote out a leader who underperforms. But this system, entwined as it is with capitalism, has gradually evolved to the point where wealth has become the fundamental power base. Private wealth, private investment, and private enterprise carry the day. Without the backing of enormous financial resources, the odds are against an individual ever winning an election.

Under the democratic political system, America's ability to act, and react, is further complicated by multiparty politics. It is an adversarial system, so it has built-in constraints that prevent the ruling party's leaders from responding to events quickly and decisively. To cite the most obvious example, the elected president in America must work with the House of Representatives and the Senate to pass major policies in an environment where fractious party politics often dominate. In addition, members of the House of Representatives face a new election every two years, which creates a built-in short-term focus. This is why their primary attention is always on getting reelected.

Here is a good example of these dilemmas in Western democracy. In August 2009, Orville Schell, director of the Center on U.S.-China relations at the Asia Society, revisited China for the sixtieth anniversary of the founding of the People's Republic of China. Schell's first trip had been in 1975, just three years after Richard Nixon became the first U.S. president to visit the PRC. (This occasion marked a historic shift for that era: the first steps toward normalizing relations between the two great nations.) Writing in the *South China Morning Post*, Schell reflected on President Barack Obama's frustrating efforts to enact change. "The U.S. Congress became paralyzed by partisan politics. Seemingly lacking a central nervous system, it has become a dysfunctional creature with little capacity to recognize any common national, much less international, interest. Under such circumstances, even a brilliant leader, with an able staff and promising policies will be unable to pursue his agenda. . . . China is veritably humming with energy, money, plans, leadership and forward motion while the West seems paralyzed."[1]

Schell went on to talk about his unique observations as he walked the streets of Beijing, ". . . the paradox that struck me was that the very system of democratic capitalism that the West has so ardently believed in and advocated now seems to be failing us. At the same time, the kind of authoritarianism and state-managed economics that we have long impugned now seems to be serving China well." Schell even speculated about where the world was headed. "It is intellectually and politically unsettling to realize that, if the West cannot quickly straighten out its systems of government, only politically unreformed states like China will be able to make the decisions that a nation needs to survive in today's high-speed, hi-tech, increasingly globalized world."

Real Politics

On the surface, politics in China would appear to be hierarchical and authoritarian. In fact, it is increasingly complex, diffuse, and quite competitive. The political process has evolved over the years. Today it is also being influenced by a myriad of entities such as ministerial bureaucracies, provincial and municipal governments, an increasing number of research groups and think tanks, the academic community, the growing private business sectors, as well as a public that is better informed with the advent of the Internet.

According to the country's constitution, the highest governing body is the National People's Congress (NPC) with its some three thousand members, but in the past it has been more of a symbolic organization endorsing proposals previously debated and ironed out by the Communist Party leadership. The real policy and decision-making entity is, in fact, the party's Politburo and its Standing Committee, comprising the two dozen or so most senior officials. It is, therefore, important to understand that despite a structural separation between the party and the state, the overlap of personnel creates a fused center of power. This makes it useful to look at the party structure and the state organs separately.

The Politburo is the most important political institution. The official head is the party's general secretary. The size and membership are determined by the Party Congress, which meets every five years. Considerable struggles and horse-trading occur before the Congress convenes, especially between the two major factions—the "princeling elitists" and the "populists"—to fill these seats of power. Since Deng's reforms, China has moved increasingly toward a collective leadership model. China's central power rests with a team given a ten-year tenure (two five-year terms). Succession would appear to be well planned and seamless, although I suspect political infighting among various factions cannot be avoided.

As a result, China is a country with one-party rule, but it is absolutely not a dictatorship. In fact, as evidence of China's evolving political system, the ruling party is no longer led by one strongman (such as Mao or Deng). Instead the Politburo and its Standing Committee are run collectively by two informal coalitions. President Hu Jintao, for example, is not a protégé of the former president, Jiang Zemin; they belonged to competing factions. This demonstrates how politics in China is no longer a zero-sum game in which a single winner takes all.

During the seventeenth Party Congress, held in 2007, four senior Politburo members (born before 1940) retired, indicating the party's adherence to agreements made for mandatory retirement at the age of sixty-eight for Politburo membership. The Standing Committee within the Politburo—a smaller group of at present nine members—is the entity that wields much of the political power. The nine people who emerged from the 2007 Congress were five returning members, including President Hu and Premier Wen, and four new faces. Two of this latter group—Xi Jinping and Li Keqiang—have now been tipped to succeed President Hu and Premier Wen respectively. Both of them were born after 1950—making them the first of the "fifth generation" of China's leadership and the only two young enough to remain in the Politburo after the upcoming Party Congress in 2012. All others will have to retire. This is why there is currently a considerable amount of political juggling between factions within the Party to fill these slots. It should also be noted that the party's secretariat is under the leadership of Vice President Xi Jinping. While it has no decision-making power, it is nevertheless the administrative arm overseeing the daily operation of the party and implementing decisions made by the Politburo and its Standing Committee.

At this point I should clarify that the Party Congress meets every five years and the National People's Congress meets every year.

The Party Congress is convened primarily to determine changes in the party's leadership. In addition, it reviews and makes changes, where necessary, to the party's constitution. It also selects the party's Central Committee of some 370 members. The Central Committee does not exercise authority as a corporate body in the same way that a legislature would. It is, however, important in that its membership is composed of leading figures of the party, the state, and the military. The Party Congress tends to be ceremonial, whereas the Central Committee meetings have often been arenas for real debate and decisions on party policy. The National People's Congress, in theory, is the highest governing body. It has, however, been more of a rubber-stamp organization, although in the recent past it appears to have become more of a forum for mediating policy differences between different parts of the party and the government.

In terms of the state or the government, the State Council is the chief authority of the country. It is appointed by the NPC, chaired by the premier, and includes the heads of each governmental department and agency. It has about fifty members, and it directly oversees all the subordinate government entities in provinces and municipalities. In practice, it maintains an interlocking membership with the top levels of the party—thus creating, as mentioned previously, a fused center of power.

Another example on this fusion of power is the Central Military Commission (CMC), which is the leading military organ and the supreme military command and decision-making body through which the Communist Party (CCP) leads the country's armed forces: the People's Liberation Army (PLA), the People's Armed Police (PAP), and the reserve forces. It basically serves both the State and the Party systems. The chairman of the CMC is elected during the Party Congress, and the post has always been held by the Party secretary-general and the country's president. Normally there are two or three vice chairmen who are uniformed officers in charge of running the CMC. It also has had a "first vice chairman" who functions as the de facto head in the daily running of the CMC. One of the vice chairmen also serves as the defense minister in the State government. In 2010, Vice President Xi Jinping, widely regarded as the next leader of China, was appointed vice chairman of the CMC—normally a signal that he is the front-runner to become the next president of the country. (For the current lineup of key leaders, please refer to Appendix A, "China's Current Leadership.")

The notion of a party controlling the government, especially when the same party effectively *is* the government, is something difficult for many in the West to accept. In China, the government and other state organs on the surface behave very much like they do in other countries. However, it is really the backstage where party forums are held and where the real politics is transacted. Under the Politburo there exists a largely secretive system that controls the entire public sector, including the military and the lives of officials who work in the various levels of government. Government ministries and agencies are staffed through an elaborate and opaque appointments system. Through behind-the-scenes committees, policy instructions are then disseminated via a government network, which guides officials in their political posture and in making public statements.

Here it is also worth looking at the process of becoming a government employee, which is very rigorous in China. Officials in public institutions are trained and retrained through approximately three thousand party schools before they are eligible for promotion. Any misconduct is first investigated by the party before being turned over to the civilian justice system. The tentacles of the state and thus the party go well beyond the government. For example, each province and each city has a party secretary who is the highest-ranking official. In terms of seniority, this official is then followed by a governor at the provincial level and a mayor at the city level. (If a party secretary shows up at a banquet together with a city mayor, for example, one must remember to toast the party secretary first.) The PLA, which is the military arm of the Communist Party of China, completes the tripartite power structure of politics, civil service, and military.

Key People

It is certainly worth examining the background of the two future leaders. They share little in terms of family background or policy orientation. Xi came from the elitist faction, which is dominated by "princelings"—the children of former high-ranking officials who grew up in the richer coastal regions and pursued careers in finance, trade, technology, and foreign affairs. His strong military ties may also serve the regime well. His connections come from two sources. His late father, Xi Zhongxun, served as the political commissar of the First Field Army on the northwestern front when the Communist forces were fighting against the KMT. His Second Field Army counterpart was none other than Deng Xiaoping, who fought in the Southwest. Later, Deng also sent him south, where he was very successful in establishing Shenzhen as the first development zone, which set the pace for China's eventual economic miracle.

The other source of connections is his own service record. He spent more than half of his working career in the coastal area facing the Taiwan Strait—from vice mayor in Xiamen to governor of the Fujian Province to governor and then party secretary of Zhejiang Province, before he was transferred to Shanghai in 2007. These local administrations all fall under the same military regime—the Nanjing regional command. Among the current leaders in CMC, many came from that command and shared a working relationship with Xi at one time or another. Well known in the international business community, he is a keen supporter of market liberalization and the continued development of the private sector. Xi will likely focus on macroeconomics and serve as China's face to the world, continuing national efforts to make the economy more efficient and global in orientation.

In contrast, Li comes from the populist faction, the members of which served in local and rural provinces and share expertise in organizational skills, propaganda, and legal affairs. His focus will be on managing social stability on the domestic front: issues such as affordable housing and health care, especially in the rural areas, as well as the plight of the country's millions of registered unemployed. Reducing disparities is more important to him than improving efficiencies in the economy.

But Xi and Li do have something important in common. They were both born after the founding of the People's Republic of China. Just teenagers when the Cultural Revolution broke out in

1966, they were sent to work as farmers: Xi in Yanan in Shaanxi Province and Li in some of the poorest rural areas in Anhui and Jiangsu Provinces. These humbling and arduous experiences helped shape their character. Today they are seen as adaptable and fore-sighted leaders armed with both endurance and humility. (Xi recently told the Chinese media that his time in Yanan was a turning point in his life.)

Two factions existing side by side within the one-party system is a significant shift in China's political landscape, and it is cer-tainly a healthy one. As leaders, Xi and Li will stand united to the public. Together they will provide a balance between economic growth and social justice. We can expect to see consensus build-ing and compromise from this new generation of leaders who will assume power in 2012. This is what I like to call "governance with Chinese characters."

While the general consensus is that Xi and Li will assume the top two positions, reliable sources also indicate that Li recently had an operation. If he doesn't make a full recovery, the premier-ship may become an open race. Should this happen, two other people are worth mentioning just for the record.

Wang Qishan is China's chief representative in the China-U.S. Strategic and Economic Dialogue, which started in 2009 and completed its third round in May 2011. Wang was born in 1948. He was governor of the China Construction Bank in the mid-nineties and later became mayor of Beijing after a brief stint as party secretary in Hainan. He became a member of the Politburo in 2007 and was made a vice premier in 2008. He is responsible for economic, energy, and financial affairs.

The other possible candidate—and in my view, the dark horse—is Wang Yang. Born in 1955, he is currently the party secretary of Guangdong Province. Prior to that, he was the party chief of Chongqing—probably one of the most important regional posi-tions in China—from 2005 through 2007. He is also a member of the Politburo and is widely regarded as a rising star among the next generation of leaders.

The changing nature of politics in China is also reflected in the world of business. The traditional state-owned enterprise (SOE) has undergone a process of corporatization. This has resulted in better-defined shareholder rights with more efficient and account-able management. I see these changes as an important part of China's continuing transition from a *planned* economy to a *market* economy. The government in many cases still controls publicly listed companies on the Shanghai or Hong Kong stock exchanges, and it still exerts considerable influence over the operations of these companies. Nevertheless, considerable improvements have been made in corporate governance.

Everything Is Possible

Unlike a Western-style democracy, policy decisions in China do not go through a tedious system of checks and balances, which partly accounts for the country's rapid economic rise in recent years. With greater maneuverability, the government can often experiment with policies on a trial-and-error basis—another example of Deng Xiaoping's saying: "Crossing the river by feeling for the stones." For example, when signs of a property bubble began to surface, the government immediately tightened bank lending and enacted vari-ous measures to cut speculative transactions. When inflation rates started to increase in 2010, interest rates were adjusted three times in a matter of four months. Lenders' required reserves were also increased several times.

Fluctuations in rules and regulations in China often frustrate Westerners, especially executives trying to do business in the coun-try. They find rapid changes to be a difficulty in making long- and even short-term plans. I often say to my Western business friends that in China everything is possible, but nothing is easy. While they spend countless hours in meetings talking about mission state-ments, positioning, and strategies, and making presentations to "visiting firemen" from head office, their Chinese competitors have already set up shop and are selling to customers!

Some opinion leaders in the West believe that division of power is the best form of governance and that for China to embrace a free market economy without a democracy would make it hard to maintain political stability. This common misunderstanding may come from a lack of knowledge about Chinese political history. For thousands of years, the rise and fall of dynasties was determined by the performance of emperors (leaders) rather than the separation of powers. In fact, according to Confucius, power cannot be separated from human character and virtue. Since 1949, when the People's Republic of China was founded after a hundred years of foreign invasions and civil wars, many scholars note that the country never fit neatly into the totalitarian, Communist, or developing country model. Perhaps it should surprise no one that in China, a growing market economy can exist without the one-person, one-vote system that defines America.

This leads us to note another important shift. When the financial crisis first surfaced in the United States a few years ago, party politics got in the way of decisions and made that government slow to react. But the problem did not just involve the House of Representatives, Senate, and executive branch. There are also a myriad of agencies, regulators, businesses, and other interest groups in this country of 310 million people. With so much consensus to be reached by so many players, it is easy to see why taking swift action is a challenge. Imagine, now, a nation such as China with more than a billion people speaking what amount to different languages and living in widely varying circumstances around the country. A proliferation of political parties would result in total chaos nationwide.

Nevertheless, Premier Wen Jiabao talked about the need for political reform in an interview with CNN's Fareed Zakaria (October 3, 2010). During his visit to New York for a session of the UN General Assembly, he met a group of Chinese media bosses on the sideline. "I've previously said economic reform without the protection of political reform will not achieve complete success and might even lose what's been gained," he said, adding, "I believe the main purpose of any political reform is to safeguard the freedoms and rights as provided under the Constitution and the law . . . to have a relaxed political environment, so people can better express their independent spirit and creativity and to allow them to enjoy free and all-round development." He went on to clarify: "I believe these should make up what we mean by democracy and freedom. In order to achieve this, we still need to have certain amount of time. This is necessitated by modern civilization and modern politics, we must work in this direction."

It is not unusual for senior Chinese leaders to speak more openly when they are traveling overseas. How far liberalization will go, however, remains to be seen. I personally do not feel that moving away from one-party rule is on the agenda. But over time, the people of China will be given more and more freedom—stopping just short of universal suffrage. In the meantime, other signs of China's internal strength are easy to see.

China's response to the economic crisis during 2009 and 2010, for example, demonstrated the flexibility of its political system. When economies in both America and Europe began to decline, China quickly adopted measures to counter the resulting slowdown in exports. A stimulus package amounting to $586 billion was spent on infrastructure and on incentives to generate more domestic consumption. Measures such as reducing import and sales taxes helped make China the largest auto market in the world. New labor policies were announced to increase the minimum wage for employees, and workers were also offered benefits such as protection for long-term service (those with tenure of ten years or more). All these policy shifts were designed to help drive domestic consumption and lessen China's reliance on exports. When signs of overheating surfaced, the central government was able to tighten bank lending to slow the economy without causing major disruptions. This quick-response capability has enabled China to weather the global downturn better than most other countries.

A more complex issue has revolved around China's currency. In 2008, the yuan had been pegged to the U.S. dollar rather than being allowed to fluctuate according to world markets. Critics argued that this move made the yuan artificially low and gave Chinese exports an unfair advantage in world trade. So they demanded that China make changes. In June 2010, the People's Bank of China, the country's central bank, announced that it would increase the flexibility of the yuan, setting the exchange rate based on market supply and demand.

This is a perfect example of a profound misunderstanding of Chinese culture. High-pressure and very public arm-twisting by U.S. officials is counterproductive because Chinese officials do not want to be seen as capitulating to foreign pressure. A more diplomatic, behind-the-scenes approach would have been far more effective in resolving this issue.

Sweeping Progress

How much has changed in China over the past half century? I am reminded that in 1972 I was a member of the first Overseas Chinese tour group from Hong Kong, which visited China shortly after Nixon's visit. Everyone we saw was dressed in either olive or faded blue Mao-style clothing. There were hardly any private vehicles, very few shops, no private property, no advertisements. The hotels we stayed in were reserved only for visitors from abroad. Whenever we left the hotel, thousands of curious onlookers gathered to stare at us as if we were from Mars. The Western-influenced hairstyles of the female members of our group attracted special attention. People approached us to feel the fabric of our clothes. Now, everything has changed or is in the process of changing.

Today, I watch in awe every time I go to China. Developments in the megacities along the coast are especially impressive. Shanghai, which is fast returning to its prewar cosmopolitan self, illustrates the transformation. The city center comprises the western (Puxi) and the eastern (Pudong) districts, separated by the Huangpu River. As recently as the early 1990s, Pudong was underused farmland and countryside. Today it is the financial center of Shanghai, characterized by landmark buildings (the Oriental Pearl Tower, the Jin Mao Building, and the Shanghai World Financial Center), shiny condos, and modern shopping malls.

In both Puxi and Pudong, imported Mercedes-Benzes and Bentleys are commonplace on the streets. Fashionably dressed consumers crowd the department stores and luxury shops (featuring Armani, Gucci, Bulgari, and LVMH), and tourists can stay at five-star international hotels such as the Four Seasons, Ritz Carlton, and Peninsula. The Peace Hotel, which hosted many celebrities and was the center of society life in the thirties, has recently undergone an elaborate renovation and just reopened under the Fairmont brand.

It is essential to realize the extraordinary scale of change. With millions and millions of Chinese striving to become millionaires— the rush of activities, the sense of urgency, and the evolution of more and more freedom—this economic tide would appear to be unstoppable. What a difference in a mere four decades. For now, the state-driven capitalist hybrid model appears to be working well for China.

Today, China and the United States are clearly the dominant world powers. In the following chapters, I document the many shifts that have led to this historic realignment. I do not propose to judge which system is better; I can see their respective strengths and weaknesses from the point of view of someone who has lived and worked for many years in both. I merely want to point out that each nation needs to understand and respect the fact that circumstances vary from country to country, especially when comparing a developed market with an emerging one. We need to look beyond national interests in favor of cooperation. In that way we will find solutions and help rescue the global economy for the benefit of everyone.

2

GUNS AND ROSES

EXPECT A ROLLER-COASTER RIDE

At a luncheon sponsored by the Asia Society in Hong Kong on June 2, 2010, the backdrop behind the podium read, "U.S.—China Relations: Rivals or Partners?" I thought to myself, should it not read "Rivals *and* Partners?" The global economy is going through an unprecedented period of uncertainty, and national and international interests are at stake. Surely the relationship between a rising China and a declining West—America in particular—will be a roller-coaster ride for the next few decades. Should we not be encouraging cooperation rather than merely looking at competition? President Hu pledged a new chapter in "cooperation as partners" during his state visit to Washington in January 2011. (See Appendix B.)

In many ways and for many reasons, China and the United States will always be rivals, because they are competing for global supremacy in the twenty-first century. But the effect of globalization also means that the two nations are interdependent. Even if their relationship is sometimes strained, an international partnership should be seen by the rest of the world as preferable to the mainly suspicious, conflict-ridden, and disconnected relationship of the past.

Signs of previous problems appear even in the language people use to talk about international relations. The term "China threat," for example, is a misnomer. Beijing has persistently tried to tell the world that it is only interested in a "peaceful rise" and in earning respect in the global arena. Examples of pursuing this goal include joining the World Trade Organization (WTO), becoming an active participant on the UN Security Council, and playing an increasing role within the World Bank and the IMF. As China's economy continues to grow and its influence expands, politicians in America worry that their country is losing its traditional position of world dominance. This partly explains why American foreign policies so often seem to be based on containment—the idea of reining in China's economic and political growth. Is this not a throwback to America's policy toward the former Soviet Union during the Cold War?

It is unnecessary to look far to see an example of this attitude. I watched in dismay as the United States once again sold arms to Taiwan in 2010 and participated in naval drills near the Korean peninsula and off the coast of Vietnam. I am also surprised that the United States would go so far as to state publicly that stability in the distant South China Sea is in its "national interest." I am of the view that this kind of disputatious behavior and language is not only exacerbating tensions between the United States and China but also wasting taxpayers' money in an era when the United States struggles with its own economy. Would it not be better to spend the money to rejuvenate old infrastructure and create badly needed jobs at home, rather than conduct drills to show off its military might? Is its power not widely known around the world?

In the meantime, China has been doing its best to help ease the North Korean situation. China has also tried to improve relations across the Taiwan Strait and negotiate bilaterally with the Association of Southeast Asian Nations (ASEAN) countries, including Vietnam, Indonesia, Malaysia, the Philippines, and Brunei, all of whom are considered friends of the United States. These negotiations have focused specifically on disputed claims over some of the islands in the South China Sea.

More recently, the East Asia Summit has grown to include a much broader representation. As a result, America, feeling left out of the process, sent Secretary of State Hillary Clinton on high-profile trips to the region to upgrade U.S. relations. The president also deployed destroyers to take part in joint military drills with

South Vietnam in China's near-coastal waters. Unfortunately, U.S. involvement only seems to complicate these already tense situations. There is no longer any need for the United States to play its traditional godfather role. We are now in a nuclear age when a large-scale war, with its potential to destroy the world, is highly unlikely. And aside from vigorously protecting its sovereignty (which explains the various border disputes) China is—in my opinion—unlikely ever to invade another country. Even if the military hierarchy were so inclined, the leaders in Beijing would insist instead on focusing efforts on China's many domestic social and political challenges. When U.S. Defense Secretary Robert Gates visited China in January 2011 to help promote a closer military-to-military dialogue with the higher echelon of the PLA, one of the stories the Western media appeared to focus on was the test flight of China's newly developed stealth fighter jet. Speculation was that this was deliberately timed to occur during the Gates visit, which China's Foreign Ministry denied. The media also reported being surprised that President Hu appeared not to know about the test flight. So the story went on to speculate about a possible rift between the Chinese military and the civilian leadership. These journalists did not address (or perhaps consider) the concept of losing face; to someone who understands Chinese culture, it seems more likely that the military wanted to make sure the test was a success before advising the leadership—but the video was somehow leaked through the Internet.

Unfortunately, the history of U.S. foreign policy toward China, as well as public opinion at a time of high unemployment, will probably compel the United States to exert pressure on China on several fronts. We will probably see more pronouncements about currency issues, trade imbalances, and border and sovereignty disputes—in part because so few high-ranking politicians in the United States fully understand China's complex circumstances. And this is not mere speculation on my part. During the U.S. midterm election in 2010, no fewer than forty candidates blamed China as part of the rhetoric in their campaign platforms.

But times have changed. China's leaders are becoming more and more confident in their country's growing power, and they are less likely to be pressured into going in a direction that could be detrimental to their country's well-being. And China is not without other support. With its economic muscle, China is cultivating relationships around the world—from Southeast Asia to Africa and Latin America. Not coincidentally, the focus is on countries with oil and natural resources that could sustain China in its economic growth. In the real world, money apparently speaks louder than words.

It was certainly unhelpful when eight U.S. lawmakers wrote a letter to the Obama administration in an effort to block the Chinese telecom firm Huawei from supplying equipment to the wireless broadband network of Sprint Nextel, the third-largest mobile operator in America. The reason? Huawei had previously sold communications technology to Iraq under Saddam Hussein. But memories are short. The United States supported Iraq during the Iran-Iraq War in the 1980s, providing billions of dollars in economic aid and supplying dual-use technology, weapons, military intelligence, and special operations training.

The letter from the lawmakers also stressed that Huawei's CEO is a former officer in the PLA. Does this mean that China should begin checking how many U.S. companies that do business in China are run by former military personnel? Firms such as Lockheed Martin, Boeing, Honeywell International, and General Electric have very close ties with the U.S. military establishment, yet they still have sizable operations in China. Incidentally, Huawei also lost a bid to acquire 2Wire, a private U.S. company that makes broadband software, because 2Wire was concerned it might lose government contracts at home. More recently Huawei also reversed a mere $2 million acquisition of a technology from 3Leaf Systems under pressure from the U.S. Committee on Foreign Investment (CFIUS). The U.S. Congress had previously blocked an attempt by a Chinese oil company to acquire a U.S. counterpart. In apparent retaliation, China blocked Coca-Cola's acquisition of a Chinese juice manufacturer on antimonopoly grounds. None of these incidents was in any way productive. I hope that Washington and Beijing will begin to favor free trade over politics going forward.

Nonetheless, Chinese companies interested in investing in the United States—especially in sectors involving technology—should pay more attention to the political environment and seek assistance with their lobbying efforts, especially in Washington, D.C. According to the Sunlight Foundation, Chinese companies spent only $425,000 on federal lobbyists in 2010—while the U.S. Chamber of Commerce, for example, spent $81 million.

Military Matters

In U.S. military circles, Admiral Robert Willard, who replaced Admiral Timothy Keating as commander of the U.S. Pacific Command in October 2009, is considered more of a hawk than his predecessor. (Movie-goers may even know that he appeared in, and was a consultant to, the 1986 Hollywood movie *Top Gun*, starring Tom Cruise.) Willard recently made some high-profile visits to the Philippines and Japan, giving press briefings along the way. Unfortunately, his comments—in my estimation—did not further good relations between the United States and China. For example, he expressed concern over China's development of an anti-ship ballistic missile—known as a carrier killer—and defended U.S. military operations in the region. "We routinely operate on both sides of the Korean Peninsula and have for 60 years," he said in Tokyo. "The nuclear-powered aircraft carrier, USS *George Washington*, has operated there as recently as last October, and the U.S. and South Korean military will continue to operate on both sides of the Korean Peninsula as circumstances dictate."[1]

The drills he referred to were reportedly aimed at North Korea, which has adamantly denied one of its submarines torpedoed a South Korean ship in March 2010, leading to heightened tensions in the area. China, however, interpreted things differently. Officials saw U.S. participation in these exercises (especially in the Yellow Sea, which is so close to Beijing) as being yet another example of a containment policy. China did nevertheless call for the resumption of the six-party talks, but the United States, South Korea, and Japan initially rejected the idea. They claimed it was merely a public relations move on the part of China. Subsequently, President Lee Myung-bak of South Korea did reconsider and at the time of this writing it is likely that the proposed dialogue will resume. All this time, the Western media blamed China for not doing enough to foster international relations in the Far East.

In September 2010, Tung Chee-hwa, Hong Kong's former chief
executive and now vice chairman of the Chinese People's Political
Consultative Conference (China's top political advisory board),
met with Admiral Willard at a dinner hosted by the U.S. con-
sul general in Hong Kong. Sources say that Tung urged Admiral
Willard against further military activity in the Yellow Sea, adding
that there was no need to fear China. Indeed, those who know
China's history will be aware that China seldom interferes with
other nations' internal affairs. China is a country that prefers to
mind its own business.

It is worth offering some background information about Tung
in the context of the escalating tensions in international waters.
Tung's family controls Orient Overseas Container Line, a leading
container shipping company. So he is knowledgeable about nau-
tical issues, from admiralty law on rights of innocent passage to
trade routes, which are the reasons the United States usually gives
for its involvement in the region. Tung lived in America in the
1960s and, partly because of his shipping background, has a wide
network of friends and associates in the United States and China.
A measure of his even-handed approach is that both sides trust
him. In January 2009, he established the nonprofit, nongovernmental China–United States Exchange Foundation to help foster
ties between the two countries. As an example of Tung's inten-
tions, the foundation sponsored a meeting between recently retired
generals from both sides (with their spouses) on Hainan Island,
hosted by retired U.S. Admiral Bill Owens, now a resident of Hong
Kong and the chair of a U.S. private equity firm.

But where Tung's foundation aims to find common ground, the
United States still sees the shift in China's power as menacing
and wants to establish itself as a regional counterweight. So, for
example, Hillary Clinton attended the East Asia Summit in Hanoi
in October 2010, while the United States and Indonesia (home
to a large Muslim population) cemented their relationship with a
pledge to expand cooperation on a global scale. The reason? They
say they can play supporting roles on hot-button issues relating
to Islam and the Middle East conflict. Clinton also indicated that
President Obama, who spent part of his childhood in Indonesia,
will be attending an East Asia Summit scheduled for Jakarta in

2011. Clinton has said that America's deeper engagement in Asia is in response to regional concerns that Washington act "as a force for peace and stability, as a guarantor of security." In other words, as the United States gradually extricates itself from Iraq, it begins turning its attention to the shift taking place in Asia—namely China's growing power and influence. The recent instability in the Middle East may affect this shift temporarily, but it seems likely to continue.

I find the aggressive behavior of the United States quite perplexing. Why does America always need to find an enemy, for example, and why is the country always acting on the pretext of safeguarding the world? Is this merely part of an effort to maintain jobs in the defense industry? Why can't America understand that, aside from border disputes, China is not outwardly aggressive, and that a partnership to address global issues is far better than wasting time and money on military maneuvers and political shadowboxing?

Partly we are seeing an old fear that power shifts can be fraught with danger. For example, in 1870, the United Kingdom not only had a military advantage over Germany but its economy was nearly three times stronger. By 1903, Germany had pulled ahead on both counts and become a threat to other European states—which eventually ended in a European war. John Mearsheimer, a realist scholar and professor of political science at the University of Chicago, has always suggested in his many articles and commentaries that the United States and China are likely to engage in intense security competition with potential for war. For example, the title of his article in *The Australian* (a newspaper) was bluntly "The Rise of China Will Not Be Peaceful at All."[2] Why is this inevitable? Not all power shifts need to result in war. In the early twentieth century, England ceded authority to the United States without any rupture in relations. Japan's rise after World War II did not challenge the existing international order. But having been invaded itself a number of times throughout history, China is hypersensitive about safeguarding its territorial rights and its sovereignty.

It may be easier to appreciate the current circumstances if you look at China's long history. Between 1839 and 1842, and again between 1856 and 1860, Britain smuggled opium from India into China in defiance of Chinese prohibition laws. When open warfare broke out between the two countries, Britain's superior military forces resulted in China's defeat, and the Qing Dynasty government was forced to sign the Treaty of Nanjing, ceding Hong Kong to Britain. The source of the problem—the opium trade—nevertheless remained. Following the decade-long Taiping Rebellion, Britain's military began a campaign that brought it to Beijing, forcing the government to sign the Treaty of Tianjin. This signaled another humiliating defeat for China.

A similar outcome can be seen in what is known as the Boxer Uprising. A militant anti-colonialist movement calling itself the Society of the Righteous Fists of Harmony declared war in 1898 on European opium traders, evangelical Christian missionaries, and other foreign influences within China. The "boxers"—as they were named by the British for their martial arts rituals—were suppressed a year later by an eight-nation alliance that stopped just short of colonizing China.

A dozen years later, China was in the midst of the 1911 Revolution. Motivated by anger toward a corrupt Qing government and repeated interventions by foreign powers, the Chinese Revolutionary Alliance clashed with the Imperial forces of the Qing Dynasty. Finally, in 1912, China was declared a republic— although internal conflicts persisted for some time. The worst was soon to follow. Fueled by China's discontent over Japan's invasion of Manchuria in 1931, a major military conflict broke out in 1937. In this instance, China received economic help from Germany, the Soviet Union, and the United States. Then, after Japan attacked Pearl Harbor on December 7, 1941, the Sino-Japanese War became an element within the much larger global conflict of World War II. In the meantime, China had to endure its own civil war.

The Civil War (also known as the War of Liberation) began in 1927. It was fought intermittently between the Western-supported Chinese Nationalist Party and the Communist Party of China, which was supported by the Soviet Union until the second Sino-Japanese War interrupted it. After World War II and in 1949, Mao Zedong established the People's Republic of China, centered in Beijing, while Chiang Kai-shek and his two million followers retreated to the island of Taiwan. Under Mao, China and its people endured years of hardship during the Great Leap Forward and the Cultural Revolution.

As a result of all this turmoil and warfare, China went through years of humiliation at the hands of foreign nations (resulting in a general mistrust of foreigners) followed by periods of domestic instability. Now, as China experiences a great shift in power and influence, national pride is also growing. But this national pride is sometimes viewed as excessive assertiveness, especially by the West at a time when U.S. influence is fading.

Both the past and the present help explain China's reaction to a variety of complex territorial issues. The following territories, for example, are claimed by both China and one or more neighboring nations:

- Taiwan
- Suyan Rock (South Korea)
- islands in the Yalu River (North Korea)
- Nansha Archipelago (Vietnam, Brunei, Malaysia, the Philippines)
- Xisha Archipelago (Vietnam)
- Huangyan Island (Philippines)
- Diaoyu Islands (Japan)
- South Tibet (India)
- Aksai Chin (India).

To China, these are seen as internal affairs in which the West has no right to interfere. When Chinese officials hear of arms sales to Taiwan, discussions with Vietnam on nuclear cooperation, military drills with South Korea, or a U.S. president meeting with the Dalai Lama, these actions are viewed as outright provocation. The Chinese see such moves as part of a containment strategy enlisting South Korea, Japan, Taiwan, the Philippines, and Vietnam to create a kind of fence around China. As Rear Admiral Yang Yi, a senior military strategist, said of Washington in August 2010, "On the one hand, it wants China to play a role in regional security issues. On the other hand, it is engaging in an increasingly tight encirclement of China and constantly challenging China's core interests."[3]

Is there any evidence to support American fears? In his 2008 book, *Strong Borders, Secure Nation: Cooperation and Conflict in China's Territorial Disputes*, U.S. political scientist M. Taylor Fravel of the Massachusetts Institute of Technology (MIT) offered a considered opinion. An authority on China's border disputes, Fravel wrote that China had offered concessions or abandoned its claims in seventeen of twenty-three territorial disputes with neighbors since 1949. In only six cases did China resort to force. This leaves the impression that, far from being an aggressive or expansionist power, China seeks stability whenever possible rather than resorting to force.[4]

Some readers may rightly recall a run-in between Chinese fishing boats and a U.S. Navy oceanographic survey ship in 2009. This is not the first time Beijing has vehemently responded to this type of operation. China regards such U.S. surveillance as both illegal and unjust. It is illegal because in China's opinion these missions violate Article 58 of the UN Convention of the Law of the Sea concerning exclusive economic zones. And the surveillance is unjust because the actions appear as an aggressive, in-your-face military intimidation by a superpower.

In a March 2009 article titled "The U.S.–China Spat at Sea," Michael Swaine of the Carnegie Endowment for International Peace said, "Don't expect China to stop harassing U.S. ships anytime soon."[5] Eric Anderson, author of *China Restored* and a leading national security consultant, wrote an open letter to President Obama in 2009 offering his opinion on surveillance: "China contends such U.S. Navy seabed mapping is really intended to facilitate submarine operations in the event of a conflict. Beijing believes such operations also serve to enhance our monitoring of Chinese submarine deployments and training." Anderson went on to clarify the difference. "To explain the Chinese sensitivities, allow me to place the shoe on the other foot. Imagine how the U.S. Department of Defense would react if the Chinese were conducting similar survey operations 75 miles off San Diego or Norfolk. I believe the term apoplectic would be appropriate should such an event come to pass."[6]

China's leadership will not forget the nation's past humiliation by outside forces. They are highly likely to take a very strong and reactionary response to any perceived foreign provocation that threatens China's sovereignty. On a more positive note, there are many examples of Chinese efforts to emphasize stability over aggression. In 1999, China signed the Southeast Asia Nuclear Weapons-Free Zone Treaty. In 2002, it agreed to the Declaration on the Conduct of Parties in the South China Sea. In 2003, China and ASEAN signed the Joint Declaration on Strategic Partnership for Peace and Prosperity to coordinate foreign and security policy. A year later, China signed a plan of action to implement the Declaration, a further sign of its intention to cooperate on matters of economics and security. Also in 2003, China entered into ASEAN's peace agreement—the Treaty of Amity and Cooperation—ahead of any other superpower. Furthermore, in 2004 China and ASEAN agreed to resolve quarrels concerning disputes in the South China Sea without the threat, or use, of force.

In the meantime, economic cooperation is likely to help with equitable settlements of disputes in the Far East. China has replaced the United States as the largest trading partner of Japan, South Korea, and Southeast Asian countries. And China and ASEAN established a free trade area that was formally launched in January 2010. It is my hope that common interests between China and ASEAN countries will override territorial disputes. At the same time, I am not naively suggesting that power and military might are not part of any nation's political priorities. While China has repeatedly emphasized a peaceful rise to power with a focus on economic growth, all countries need to build up their military capabilities as a form of self-defense.

It would appear that China's idea is to leapfrog American military hardware by developing high-tech, close-in weapons targeting America's reliance on communications and intelligence technology. The intention is to provide a safety net around China's coastal region (including Taiwan) without purchasing millions of tons of new hardware in a race to reach parity with the United States. So, despite China's defense budget rising to become the second highest in the world behind the United States, it is important to remember that China's 6.6 percent share of global expenditure on arms is dwarfed by America's 46.5 percent share. Stated even more simply, America spends more on defense than the rest of the industrialized world combined. The question in this age of dramatic shifts in power, influence, and economic fortunes is not whether China poses a danger but whether the United States will remain such a dominant force.

Meanwhile, on the global stage, some human rights advocates, academics, and officials in the West have raised concerns about China's sale of weapons to dictatorships such as Sudan and Zimbabwe. They are effectively saying that Beijing is undermining the development of democracy and rights in Africa. However, a study coauthored by Paul Midford and Indra de Soysa, using data compiled by the Stockholm International Peace Research Institute, has turned common wisdom on its head. People naturally assume that because China is an authoritarian state, it will want to sell arms to other authoritarian states and that the U.S. will do the opposite. The truth is that Russia sold five times more arms to Khartoum than China, according to the Stockholm data. Beijing's sales to Egypt, for example, were dwarfed by those of the United States, which provided Egypt with billions of dollars' worth of fighter jets, tanks, and missiles.

None of these arguments are meant to excuse Chinese arms sales to undemocratic regimes. My point is simply that the West is selling a lot more military weaponry to the same countries. As a result, it is unfair to paint a picture of China as a military threat or a war-mongering nation. In fact, China is far more focused on a daily basis on its economic fortunes—seeking resources to sustain economic growth at home.

Fortunately, some of the media in the United States are willing to give voice to that opinion. In late 2010, Helene Cooper, a White House correspondent for the *New York Times,* wrote in the *International Herald Tribune*:

> A fundamental tenet of foreign policy says that nations will seldom voluntarily act against what they have determined, for whatever reason, to be their own national interest. Somebody

needs to tell that to the United States when it comes to China. . . .

A key part of the United States relationship with China now turns on a question that is, at its heart, an impossible conundrum: How to get Beijing to make moves that its leaders do not think are good for their country? Beijing has resisted letting its currency rise because it depends on a cheap Renminbi to drive its export-heavy economy. China has balked at stiff sanctions to rein in Iran's nuclear ambitions because it needs access to Iran's oil and gas fields to fuel its own growth. . . . And Beijing has recoiled at reining in its unruly neighbor to the East . . . because it does not want to destabilize North Korea to an extent that could lead to the government's collapse.

China will not bite on a host of issues, some experts say, until the U.S. changes not only its tactics but the entire way that the U.S. Government views Beijing.[7]

Having dominated the world as the sole superpower for so long, many U.S. officials still harbor the belief that other nations must go along with America's worldview. With China's rise, this mindset will need to change as the world will move increasingly toward a multipower system. This will require future diplomacy to be negotiated on equal terms.

Looking Ahead

President Hu's state visit to the United States in January 2011 could certainly be viewed as an example of "power diplomacy." He and President Obama both agreed to share expanding common interests and pledged closer cooperation on a wide range of areas such as trade, energy, environmental protection, and intellectual property rights. At the post-summit news briefing as reported by *China Daily* on January 21, 2011, President Hu said, "We both agreed to further push forward the positive, cooperative and comprehensive China-U.S. relationship and commit to work together to build a partnership based on mutual respect and mutual benefit so as to better benefit people in our own countries and the world over." He added that a strategic long-term perspective will ensure relations will not be affected or held back by any one incident at any particular time. President Obama indicated that he absolutely believes China's peaceful rise is good for the world and good for America, saying, "We've shown that the U.S. and China, when we cooperate, we can [all] receive substantial benefits."

A series of trade deals were also unveiled, including China's purchase of two hundred Boeing aircraft. The $45 billion deals, according to U.S. officials, would support 235,000 American jobs.

China and Europe

Lest we overlook the other part of the West, perhaps a good example would be President Hu's state visit to France and Portugal in November 2010. As Paris prepares to take over the G20 presidency, the once-rocky relationship between the two world powers appeared to be returning to the closeness of the de Gaulle era. President Hu and President Sarkozy inked deals totaling 16 billion euros ($22.8 billion), which included 102 Airbus planes, telecom equipment, and 20,000 tons of uranium. Local French authorities also announced that a new 500 million-euro French-Chinese business district will be established in Chateauroux in Central France—creating some four thousand jobs. In the meantime, China also bought both Portuguese and Spanish sovereign bonds to help bring back some investors' confidence to these troubled countries. Yi Gang, deputy governor of the People's Bank of China, told the *Guardian*, "We have been a consistent buyer and we have a long-term view of our investments in Europe."[8] China said it was in its own interests to support the EU in times of trouble as the economic bloc is China's top trading partner.

Hope

As we begin the second decade in the twenty-first century, let's hope we will see more roses and fewer guns.

3

THE CHINESE PIGGY BANK

THE GLOBAL SHIFT IN ECONOMIC RELATIONS

My grandfather was a firm believer in an old Chinese motto: *If you cannot buy something with cash then you cannot afford it.* Living on credit is not acceptable. We need to save money for the things we want. This lesson was drummed into me at an early age, and I have since passed this on to my children. Having a high level of personal savings is an integral part of the Chinese culture. Generations of Chinese endured hardship and poverty. Families tend to do everything possible to build a nest egg for the future of their children and for their old age, because in China social programs such as health care and pension schemes still do not provide for everyone's needs.

There are probably several other reasons why the personal savings rate is between 25 and 30 percent of the GDP—and the national savings rate is between 45 and 50 percent. Ever since China's one-child policy was introduced in 1978, families have tended to favor sons. Some parents would even decide to abort if a female fetus was detected through ultrasound. As a result, there are roughly 122 boys to every 100 girls in China, although this figure may be overstated as girls born in rural areas may not have been registered. (In contrast, the average in industrialized countries is 107:100.) Families with boys are inclined to save more so that their sons will have a competitive advantage in finding a spouse.

Although things are changing, an underdeveloped banking and financial services sector was another factor that encouraged saving by making it difficult to borrow for housing, education, and medical care.

Today, two factors have altered this picture. First, the Bank of China introduced the country's first credit card in 1985, although the industry remained tiny until about 2002 when credit cards were reintroduced in a significant way along with an infrastructure to support their use. In September 2010, MasterCard predicted that by the end of the decade, China would overtake the United States as the world's largest market for credit cards, with about 900 million in circulation. Second, the central government will continue to push for increased domestic consumption, designed to offset slowdowns in exports caused by the economic decline of the West. At the same time, concern for the future has lessened as the government continues to improve social security programs. It is now likely that younger generations will soon become more active consumers, and the level of materialism common to Western democracies will be the reality in China as well.

In the meantime, the attitude of citizens in the West, and the United States in particular, continues to be "Enjoy now and worry about paying later." This is a habit—perhaps I should call it an addiction—that will be hard to reverse. Financial institutions also encourage their clients to leverage themselves. You must have a credit rating to be able to make a lot of transactions in the United States. But how do you get a credit rating? The simple answer is that you have to borrow, whether it is through the use of credit cards, applying for home mortgages, or buying cars and appliances on installment plans.

This system worked reasonably well as long as jobs were available and wages continued to rise. But that was before the financial crisis of 2008. In the years that followed, rising unemployment levels, triggered partly by globalization, encouraged companies around the world to seek lower-cost labor in emerging markets to sustain their profitability. Manufacturing jobs in the United States and Europe have been disappearing, many of them permanently. China, with its hardworking cheap labor force, benefited from globalization as Western multinationals, under pressure from their shareholders to maximize quarterly profits, flocked to China in search of lower costs of production.

Easy Target

All this may explain the various economic forces at work. But for America, which currently seems to be lacking other solutions, the loss of domestic jobs has inevitably become politicized. When looking for a scapegoat, Americans and their politicians find China an easy target. As noted earlier, during the November 2010 mid-term elections, dozens of U.S. candidates reportedly spent millions of dollars on attack ads. These politicians were suggesting that Americans have suffered because their opponents have been sympathetic to China. (They typically used unambiguous imagery and audio, ranging from a dragon to Mao coupled with Chinese music.) One Democratic congressman, Zack Space, accused his Republican opponent, Bob Gibbs, of supporting free-trade policies that sent to China jobs that otherwise would have gone to Ohioans. As a giant dragon appeared across the screen, the narrator said: "As they say in China, *xie xie Mr. Gibbs.*" [Thank you, Mr. Gibbs.][1]

Many of these politicians chose to ignore the rational truth in favor of pursuing votes at any cost. Either way, they argued that increasing the value of the yuan against the dollar would keep jobs in America. Chinese officials and some economists (both in China and in the West) tried to remind people about the Japanese yen in the 1980s. At that time, Americans were upset over an increase in Japanese imports, just as they are unhappy with Chinese imports today. The United States pushed Japan to let the yen appreciate and Japan complied, allowing its currency to surge by some 50 percent between 1985 and 1987. Instead of improving the situation, the trade deficit actually widened. The moral of the story is that even a sharp rise in the Chinese yuan may not do much to help the U.S. economy. It would merely make many day-to-day items more expensive for American consumers. In fact, the yuan actually rose 21 percent against the U.S. dollar between 2005 and 2008, yet the trade deficit continued to rise.

The Peterson Institute, a Washington-based think tank, estimates the yuan is undervalued by 25–40 percent, thus subsidizing

Chinese exports and taxing its imports at the expense of other countries. China, on the other hand, says its currency policy is an internal matter, driven by the need to maintain economic growth and provide jobs, which relates to China's perpetual concern for maintaining social stability. What so many of its critics never seem to understand is that openly labeling China a "currency manipulator" is always going to be counterproductive. Today, China has become an economic power, and a proud country that attaches so much importance to *guanxi* (relationships) cannot be seen in the international arena as having capitulated under pressure from the United States.

International Developments

Ultimately, China is likely to revalue the yuan, since rebalancing the world's economy would help global economic recovery and create global stability, but it will do so on a gradual basis. In the meantime, China will continue to hold other trump cards.

Controlling the export of rare earth minerals crucial to manufacturing many advanced high-tech products—such as cellphones, wind turbines, automobiles, and even guided missiles—is but one example.

The timing of China's announcement about export control measures over new rare earth minerals in the fall of 2010 was unfortunate. The West interpreted this news as China trying to force Japan to release a fishing boat captain who had been arrested because his boat collided with a Japanese coast guard vessel near the Diaoyu Islands. China denied it was using this as a political tool, but in the real world it is true that companies and nations are always on the lookout for a competitive advantage. It is also possible that as China's manufacturing sectors continue to grow, demand for rare earth minerals as raw materials is also on the increase domestically.

Beijing may often be running China like a corporation, but the top priority is still to maintain stability within the country, so every change is undertaken gradually. China would never adjust its currency abruptly—say by 20 percent as some U.S. politicians have advocated—because a slowdown in exports would cause a significant loss of jobs and a flight of capital to other emerging markets with cheaper labor costs. (Not to mention increased currency speculation and exchange losses on hundreds of billions in the debt China holds for the U.S. Treasury.)

One solution would be if the United States allowed the sale of advanced technology, which China is eager to buy. But so far Washington has blocked the sale of items such as sensors, optics, and biological and chemical processes that might have military applications on the grounds of national security. Some suggest not all items on the U.S. "forbidden list" are truly matters of national security, and if America would relax its restrictions, this would go a long way to addressing the trade imbalance with China.

In late 2010, as China promised financial aid to the European Union's debt-ridden countries in an effort to help the global economic recovery, it also called on the EU to lift restrictions on exports of high-tech products. European leaders understandably welcomed the high-profile visit of Vice Premier Li Keqiang in January 2011 as he pledged to diversify China's foreign currency reserves away from low-yielding U.S. Treasury debt into euro-denominated debt. As a result, yields on the government bonds of Spain, Portugal, and Greece began to rise. China needs to support the euro, because a weaker euro would work against it by making high-quality goods produced in countries like Germany more affordable on world markets and therefore give Chinese exports more competition. Li also presided over several business accords, among them one between Repsol, the largest Spanish oil company, and China Petrochemical to expand oil exploration in Latin America, where China would like to continue to grow its investments.

In my view, China should make every effort to push for the internationalization of the yuan. Beijing should try to increase the yuan's proportion in international settlements, develop it into one of the strongest investment currencies in the global financial market, and eventually forge it into a leading reserve currency. For example, cross-border yuan trade settlements are now allowed in all countries and regions of the world, after beginning first in Hong Kong, Macao, and the ten ASEAN member states in 2009. Many enterprises in China can now settle their merchandise imports, service trades, and other current account transactions in yuan, while an increasing list of eligible enterprises will be able to settle their merchandise exports in that currency. The share of bank deposits denominated in yuan in Hong Kong quadrupled in 2010. Seventy thousand Chinese companies are now doing their cross-border settlements in yuan. Dozens of foreign multinationals have issued yuan-denominated "dim sum" bonds in Hong Kong. In January 2011, the Bank of China also began offering yuan-deposit accounts in New York insured by the Federal Deposit Insurance Corporation.

In August 2010, the People's Bank of China, the country's central bank, announced that it would allow overseas financial institutions to invest in the country's interbank bond market on a trial basis in an effort to further promote yuan cross-border trade settlements. In the immediate future, however, China should actively set up channels for the yuan's foreign investment. It should reduce its debt investments and instead increase equity investments. State-owned companies and sovereign wealth funds have already shown increasing interest in making direct investments into companies not only in the United States but throughout the world. For example, China Investment Corporation, a $300 billion sovereign wealth fund, has been an active buyer of equity stakes in the Canadian mining firm Teck Resources ($3.54 billion), along with such North American giants as Blackstone ($3 billion), Morgan Stanley ($1.77 billion), Citigroup ($29.8 million), Bank of America ($19.9 million), Coca-Cola ($9 million) and Apple ($6.3 million).

As for America, one must remember that the United States trade deficit is global, and not only restricted to China. As David D. Hale and Lyric Hughes Hale wrote in *Foreign Affairs* early in 2008: "China is but one cog, and revaluation just one lever, in the complex machinery of international trade."[2] From Beijing's point of view, there are well over 100 million manufacturing jobs in China (compared to perhaps 15 million in the United States) Beijing, therefore, is obviously concerned that any significant appreciation in the yuan could reduce employment in China, resulting in social instability. With wages rising in the prosperous coastal regions, Beijing has also mounted a push inland to the western parts of the country—not only to close the wealth gap but to make it possible for migrant workers to work closer to home, which in turn would distribute local consumption more evenly across the country.

Still, the rate of savings in China remains comparatively high, as outlined earlier, because this habit is a holdover from the days when individual preparations had to be made to fund health care, retirement, and the education of children. The government has therefore stepped up improvements in both health care and pensions to encourage people to save less and spend more. The Chinese piggy bank, which includes personal, corporate, and government savings, has also enabled Beijing to build an elaborate infrastructure of roads and railways (particularly high-speed rail). This is part of an overall policy to unite the country, including bringing the Tibetan and Xinjiang autonomous regions closer into the mainstream of Chinese life.

Beijing is also trying to slow the growth in foreign exchange reserves. For example, over the years mainland Chinese have been granted more freedom to purchase Hong Kong equities. Chinese companies are also making overseas acquisitions. By reducing the reserves, China hopes to bring its economy more into equilibrium. One high-profile move by the state-controlled China National Offshore Oil Corporation (CNOOC) was its effort to acquire Unocal, the ninth-largest oil company in the world. The bid failed over U.S. political and national security concerns, but CNOOC, undaunted by the experience, then offered to buy a one-third stake in Chesapeake Energy's shale oil and gas acreage in southern Texas for $1.08 billion. To sweeten the deal, it committed to spending another $1.08 billion to shoulder 75 percent of drilling and other development costs. This deal was completed in November 2010, and it marked the first major investment by a Chinese state-run company in onshore energy reserves in the United States. The formal announcement was made by Chesapeake Energy and CNOOC, both of which are listed on the New York Stock Exchange. Aubrey McClendon, Chesapeake's CEO, commented, "We are very pleased to have partnered with CNOOC Ltd. in completing our fifth industry shale development transaction. We look forward to accelerating the development of this large domestic oil and natural gas resource, resulting in a reduction of our country's oil imports over time, the creation of thousands of high-paying jobs in the U.S. and the payment of very significant local, state and federal taxes."[3] ConocoPhillips also sold 9 percent of Syncrude Canada to Sinopec International Petroleum Exploration and Production Company of China for $4.65 billion. The sale was part of Conoco's effort to strengthen its financial position and improve its return on capital investment. Syncrude is the world's largest producer of light sweet crude oil from oil sands.[4]

In the technology sector, Alibaba.com (listed on the Hong Kong Stock Exchange) acquired Auctiva, a Chico, California-based company, which is the leading third-party developer of tools for eBay, in August 2010. With more than 170,000 active users, Auctiva provides a variety of listing, marketing, and management tools as well as image hosting and online store fronts that make it easier for small businesses to sell successfully via e-commerce on sites like eBay. Alibaba also acquired Vendio, headquartered in San Mateo, California, in June. These acquisitions together with Alibaba's strength in sourcing will create a significant package of tools for small businesses looking to leverage e-commerce. The combination brings more than 250,000 new customers to the Alibaba.com family of products and significantly expands Alibaba's footprint in the United States.[5]

Besides energy and technology sectors, other Chinese companies are also on the prowl. For example, Bright Food (Group), a Shanghai-based conglomerate, has been in exclusive talks with Blackstone of the United States and PAI Partners of France, the private equity firms that control the British company United Biscuits. Unlike the sale of the British firm Cadbury to U.S.-owned Kraft Foods early in 2010, which caused a political storm in Britain, this deal seems unlikely to spark a similar nationalist uproar, because United Biscuits is already in foreign hands. With both Campbell Soup and Kraft also showing interest, however, latest indications are that all or part of United Biscuits may now go through the auction process.

U.S. Response

The U.S. Congress passed a bill during the midterm elections in November 2010 permitting the U.S. government to impose tariffs on Chinese exports in retaliation for China's purported currency manipulation. This is the kind of initiative that should not get past the Senate (although if it did, President Obama would veto it), because aggressive and public moves such as these will only end up in trade wars, with China retaliating in kind. A trade war would not benefit citizens around the world and would only serve to heighten the blame game.

To put all this in perspective, recall that in the 1930s it was a rising tide of worldwide protectionism that put the global economy into a death spiral. If changes in the exchange rate are truly so significant, then the U.S. trade deficit with China should have decreased during the period from 2005 to 2008 when the yuan was revalued by some 20 percent. Instead, the trade deficit continued to grow. The real problem is America's deteriorating competitiveness and its shortfall in savings. Instead of helping to stimulate the local national economy, America's quantitative easing program in 2010 resulted in massive liquidity in emerging markets in Asia.

Not surprisingly, both the World Bank and the IMF expressed concerns. A wave of money flooding into emerging markets in Asia could undermine the region's export competitiveness, destabilizing exchange rates, pumping up inflation, and creating asset bubbles. Policymakers in Asia need to learn the lessons from the Asian financial crisis of 1997–98, when an influx of global capital inflated property and equity prices, only to collapse when the money flows reversed. Whether this was a deliberate ploy by the United States, I will leave to global financial experts to judge.

China's U.S. Treasury holdings are now over $900 billion, and China is Washington's number one creditor. There is, however, a dilemma because China's huge foreign investment is in the form of reserve assets, or government lending, as opposed to foreign direct and private investments. China's large-scale purchases of U.S. government bonds may get only a 3 or 4 percent return. On the other hand, the United States, despite its huge debt and trade deficit, accepts more dollar inflow and turnaround and then invests these commodity dollars into the emerging Asian markets—getting a return of 10 to 15 percent. Since China cannot use its own currency to issue debt, its swollen trade surplus could intensify the risk of a devaluation in its reserve assets. As a result, the United States is using its debtor status as an unchecked instrument to maintain its hegemony in the global financial domain. The so-called dollar standard not only helped the United States circulate its national debt globally, it also helped increase its national wealth through monetization of U.S. government debt, or depreciation of the dollar.

Almost half of the world's international trade is settled in dollars. More than 60 percent of the foreign reserves held by other countries are in dollars, and the dollar is used approximately 85 percent of the time in international financial transactions. As the distributor of the world's leading currency, the United States can simply print more money to boost its ability to pay off its inflated national debt. The dollar's devaluation has clearly been used as a major means to reduce U.S. government debt, and no matter how large the Chinese piggy bank grows, it is no match for the output of freshly printed American bills.

As a side note, let me share an interesting story. Stephen Roach, a world-renowned chief economist with New York financial giant Morgan Stanley, lived in Hong Kong for several years as head of the firm's global team of economists. He once attended a U.S. Congressional hearing and tried to explain that America should not blame China for the high unemployment in the United States. Roach argued that America has lost its competitiveness, and that its trade deficit was with countries *around* the world, not just China. Many manufacturing jobs will never return to America, he explained, and if they had not migrated to China they would be in India or Indonesia or Vietnam. At the end of the hearing, resorting to the equivalent of a schoolyard taunt, one of the commission members called him a "Panda Hugger."

That is politics!

Building the Private Sector

China's private sector certainly played an important role in helping the country navigate through the financial crisis. The Chinese word for business, *sheng yi*, translates as "create new meanings," and that is exactly what China has done by embracing private enterprise. After all, just a few decades ago the country's social and cultural environment was hostile toward it. Banks would not lend money to private businesses, and this sector was viewed suspiciously as the antithesis of Confucian teachings and a tool of Western capitalism.

But then Beijing amended its constitution in 1999 so the private sector could be formally recognized, setting the stage for the radical changes visible today. According to statistics released early in 2011 by China's State Administration of Industry and Commerce, the number of individual enterprises in China increased to more than 40 million, providing more than 160 million jobs. Private companies now account for 74 percent of China's businesses, and the total registered funds associated with the private sector were nearly $3 trillion by the end of 2010, with an accumulated growth rate of more than 150 percent between 2005 and 2010.

In addition, private Chinese enterprises exported goods valued at $481.3 billion in 2010, according to a 2011 report by the All-China Federation of Industry and Commerce (ACFIC). That represents an increase of 255 percent over 2005. "Without the stable and healthy development of the private sector," says Huang Mengfu, chairman of the ACFIC, "China has no possibility of substantially achieving economic restructuring."[6]

And where China's private enterprises were once associated mainly with overseas investment in economically underdeveloped countries in Africa and Latin America, increasingly they are expanding into mature markets such as North America, Europe, Japan, and South Korea. They are also making a transition from focusing mainly on mineral and energy resources to more sophisticated areas such as electronic communications.

But the development of China's private sector has some inherent weaknesses. Today, the country has a hybrid economy, neither fully communist nor fully capitalist, run by a government that has evolved away from genuine top-down central control yet is not subject to the kinds of constitutional checks and balances associated with Western democracies. Integrating the private sector into the country's socialist market economy continues to be a huge and complex transition. Banks still favor lending to the big, state-owned companies because they have government backing.

"China has a long history and a splendid culture, but the market economy is a completely imported concept," said Wu Jia Yuan, in an interview with *China Knowledge at Wharton*, a business research journal of the Wharton School at the University of Pennsylvania. "We know very little about how to develop a business and compete in a market economy."

Wu is a private entrepreneur who rose to chairman of Hubei Dengfeng Heat Exchanger Company, a $73 million firm that serves the petrochemical, marine, mining, and automotive industries, among others. In the interview, he added: "Furthermore, impatience is widespread in China, and if manifested in company management, it leads to a host of issues and potential crises [affecting] a company's growth and survival."[7]

Wu's cautionary words are echoed by Barry Naughton, the So Kwanlok Chair of Chinese International Affairs at the Graduate School of International Relations and Pacific Studies at the University of California, San Diego. Naughton, who has believed for years that China will become an economic powerhouse influencing the world in hitherto unimagined ways, authored a 2007 book called *The Chinese Economy: Transitions and Growth*. In it, he wrote:

> Ultimately, China's diversity can be traced to two incomplete transitions. First, China is still completing its transition away from bureaucratic socialism [Maoism-Stalinism] and toward a market economy. Second, China is in the middle of the industrialization process, the protracted transformation from a rural to an urban society. China is in the midst of "economic development," the process that transforms every aspect of an economy, society, and culture. These two transitions are both far from complete, and so China today carries with it parts of the traditional, the socialist, the modern, and the market, all mixed up in a jumble of mind-boggling complexity.[8]

Financial Crisis

In 2008, the UN General Assembly on Reforms of the International Monetary and Financial System set up a commission of experts to examine the global financial crisis and suggest reforms. The commission was chaired by Professor Joseph Stiglitz, a Nobel Prize winner and a former chief economist at the World Bank. Members of the commission included three Central Bank governors, several former and current finance ministers and other currency experts. The preliminary report began with the following statement in its preamble:

> The rapid spread of the financial crisis from a small number of developed countries to engulf the global economy provides tangible evidence that the international trade and financial system needs to be profoundly reformed to meet the needs and changed conditions of the 21st Century. Past economic crises have had a disproportionate adverse impact on the poor, who are least able to bear these costs, and that can have consequences longer after the crisis is over.[9]

Four days later, Chinese Central Bank governor Zhou Xiaochuan presented a paper on the bank's website titled "Reform the International Monetary System." It questioned the U.S. dollar's role and argued for its replacement by another kind of currency unit, which should not be that of one country but should stand above all others as a kind of supranational currency. The *Financial Times* commented:

> China yesterday threw down a challenge to America's 50-year dominance of the global economy as it proposed replacing the dollar as the world's main reserve currency with a new global system under the control of the International Monetary Fund (IMF). In a muscle-flexing move that will be seen as an attempt to exploit the big shifts in economic power created by the recession sweeping the West, Beijing said that the dollar's role could eventually be taken over by the IMF's so-called Special Drawing Right (SDR), a quasi-currency that was created in 1969 . . . . China's central bank governor has delivered a powerful message to the world. He wants an end to the dollar era. This is not sabre-rattling. He has made serious proposals for a reserve currency to rival the greenback and he deserves a hearing . . . . Beijing now wants to play an active role in reshaping the world's monetary order. This outward looking view should be welcomed.[10]

U.S. Treasury Secretary Tim Geithner's initial reaction was, "it deserves some consideration." The dollar fell sharply against the euro and other major currencies, prompting Geithner to issue a same-day clarification indicating the dollar would remain the world's dominant reserve currency for some time to come.

On January 13, 2011, China launched a pilot program to allow domestic Chinese companies to use Chinese currency overseas to make overseas investments. This is part of China's efforts to make the yuan a global currency. The Central Bank also set the yuan's reference rate at a new high against the dollar, coming in the run-up to President Hu's state visit to the United States. The yuan has now risen by 3.4 percent since it was effectively depegged to the U.S. dollar in June 2010. In recent months, China has made efforts to encourage the yuan's use outside China—further relaxing its grip to become less dependent on the dollar for trade and investment.

It is interesting to note that at the beginning of the decade, U.S. banks dominated rankings—measured as a bank's share price as a multiple of its book value. Four of the top five were Bank of New York Mellon, Morgan Stanley, Citigroup, and Wells Fargo. (Lloyds of London was the fifth one.) In contrast, in 2009 the top four banks were all Chinese: China Merchants Bank, China CITIC Bank, ICBC, and China Construction Bank. The highest ranked U.S. bank—U.S. Bancorp—was number fifteen. Times have changed, and so have the concentrations of wealth and power in the world.[11]

As global power shifts, the world's financial system remains the fundamental element driving prosperity and wealth. Rather than politicizing currency and exchange rates, the United States and China should take the lead to work on a stable global financial and monetary system. With China's projected economic growth set to eventually match that of the United States as well as the Euro zone, and with cautious and sound macroeconomic management, the yuan will be a promising candidate to become the third stabilizing leg of the international monetary system.

Although many Americans may not realize it, China is willing to share power with the United States. Today, China's internal financial markets tend to be overly controlled, but its economy is now larger than Japan's and growing faster. And with the size of its reserves, China will play a far more influential role going forward. China, on its own, cannot bring an end to the U.S. dollar's global dominance. However, if it adds its weight to a growing consensus, it will affect the outcome.

4

NOT MADE IN CHINA

WHY THE U.S. TRADE DEFICIT WITH CHINA IS NOT WHAT IT SEEMS

When I first set foot in America in 1954, the nation was in the middle of a decade of postwar transition. William Levitt, the legendary real estate developer, had just pioneered the modern subdivision with his Long Island development known as Levittown. As the trend caught on and more suburban communities were built, families migrated to homes that were within easy commuting distance of major cities. Suddenly these new bedroom communities had their own Parent Teacher associations, Boy and Girl Scout organizations, and Little League baseball. Backyard barbecues and cocktail parties were popular social events. The first enclosed shopping mall—Southdale Center, in a suburb outside Minneapolis—opened in 1956. The suburban development trend also benefited the automobile industry as cars became necessities for everyone.

These were the baby boom years. In less than a decade, half of all American households owned a TV set, and families were glued to the tube an average of six hours a day watching popular shows such as *I Love Lucy* and *Gunsmoke*. (That is why the TV dinner was invented around the same time.) Television also allowed the public to be closer to the political fabric of the country; the nation watched the Army-McCarthy hearings in 1954 and, in 1960, the four presidential debates involving John F. Kennedy and Richard Nixon leading up to the widely watched election night triumph for the charismatic Kennedy.

That was more or less the beginning of "Made in America" or "Made in U.S.A.," a label that represented not only quality but also prestige. Products ranging from clothing to shoes to household products and cars as well as food, beverages, and personal care items were in demand around the world. As it happened, rumor had it that there was a town in Japan called Usa. Some unscrupulous company back then actually made products there with the label "Made in USA" (without the dots in between the letters) and tried to pass off these items as genuine "Made in U.S.A." products. In those days, products that read "Made in U.S.A." were truly made in America, from extraction of the raw materials through production and assembly to finished product. Today, however, when products carry a "Made in China" label, they are really just "Assembled in China"—an important point I return to later in the chapter.

Fast-forward fifty years. Today, whenever I visit my grandchildren in California, one of the highlights is our trip to retailing giant Target to buy toys. I limit them to picking out two items each within a certain budget, which means they spend many agonizing minutes—sometimes as long as an hour—trying to decide what to buy. This coincidentally allows me the opportunity to check out products on nearby shelves.

With my background in consumer marketing, I always enjoy looking at new products, from men's and women's clothing to electronic items to various day-to-day necessities. I am always amazed at how many of the products carry a "Made in China" label. Most of them, in fact. And the others might read "Made in Sri Lanka," "Made in Indonesia," "Made in Philippines" or "Made in Vietnam." These outings often remind me of *A Year Without Made in China: One Family's True-Life Adventure in the Global Economy*, a book by Sara Bongiorni. After yet another Christmas awash in plastic toys and electronic gear, Bongiorni decided to live for one year without buying any products made in China. What Bongiorni found out was that while living without

"Made in China" is possible, it is a lot of trouble: inconvenient, if not unrealistic, and likely to cut into a family's budget.[1]

But why would a Westerner want to boycott Chinese products? Almost certainly because of a commonly held misconception: the idea that China's actions result in lost jobs in America. And this is patently untrue. For one thing, many of the factory jobs performed by people in China would be done by machines in America. For another, increases in productivity because of technological innovations, improvements in inventory management, and other advances mean that manufacturers in the United States can earn more with less overhead, including payroll costs.

Although Americans sometimes equate "Made in China" with cheap, junky goods, the West relies on China for a lot of products that are not poorly made. In fact, Chinese exports form the basis of contemporary consumer culture: computers, smart phones, wall-sized flat-screen TVs, cameras, camcorders, GPS systems, portable e-book readers, and other modern essentials. Blaming China for manufacturing woes in America simply does not make sense. The United States remains the world's leading manufacturer by value of goods produced. For every dollar of value produced in China, the United States generates $2.50. In large part, this is because American corporations have shifted toward higher-end manufacturing (auto parts, farm machinery, gas turbines for power plants, computer chips). This is why Chinese officials will say that huge surpluses showing up in trade statistics overstate their country's prosperity. While these statistics look good on paper, in fact it is the foreign companies—including many American ones—that reap the largest profits.

In a *New York Times* article published early in 2006, Dong Tao, an economist at UBS in Hong Kong, was quoted as saying: "In a globalized world, bilateral trade figures are irrelevant. The trade balance between the U.S. and China is as irrelevant as the trade balance between New York and Minnesota."[2] In other words, we are all part of one large and interconnected web of trading, and it does little good to point fingers and say that one party is taking advantage of another. As Dong Tao suggests, we are all in this together.

Building Industry

China's modern period of industrialization began in the late 1970s, when former Communist Party leader Deng Xiaoping began reforming the country's economy and opening it up to the world—blending communism and capitalism on the pragmatic grounds that "It doesn't matter whether the cat is black or white so long as it catches mice." At that time, Shenzhen, which is in Guangdong Province immediately north of Hong Kong, was a fishing town of around 75,000 people (practically a village by Chinese standards).

In 1980, Shenzhen became the first special economic zone, where the limitations of a planned economy no longer applied. Chinese and foreign investors were lured there with low taxes, inexpensive land, cheap labor, and relative economic freedom. As a result, many Chinese entrepreneurs from Hong Kong, Taiwan, and other Asian countries began to build factories that made a wide range of products on an OEM basis for export to the United States and Europe. (Original equipment manufacturers, or OEMs, are companies that make products for others to package and resell under their own brand names.) Many joint ventures were also formed, often with U.S.-based multinationals.

Shenzhen recorded a growth rate that exceeded 40 percent annually for years. With an influx of migrant workers from all over China, its population grew a hundred times over three decades, to reach 14 million today. For a while, the government had to limit the inpouring of migrants looking for employment by issuing work permits. So new factories began to locate further inland to places such as Dongguan, which has four township-level divisions and twenty-eight towns within its administration. Being north of Shenzhen, workers here do not require permits. This whole region eventually became what many called simply "the factory for the world," because international companies could lower their costs by having their products made—or, to be more precise, I should say *assembled*—here.

This qualification of "assembling" is critically important. The management of U.S. and European companies, under pressure from Wall Street analysts and demanding shareholders, must continuously be on the lookout for ways to lower their costs. With globalization, companies also buy raw materials wherever they can get the best price. That means most products are manufactured with materials from around the world, assembled in China, and then shipped to their ultimate markets in the West. So America's trade deficit is with *many* countries around the world, not just China. In fact, the value added in China's exports is marginal, not nearly as significant a part of the overall GDP as some may think.

For example, consider a product that sells for $100 in the United States. I would calculate that no more than 10 percent, and often much less, of that would be likely to stay in China, representing labor for assembling the product, while perhaps another 10 percent would represent materials imported from various parts of the world. So about 80 percent of the retail cost of the product goes to the brand owner, which will cover distribution costs, advertising and marketing expenses, and other administrative costs in addition to profits. (The actual profit margin will vary depending on factors such as competition in the product category, the brand owner's policies, and economic circumstances in that country.)

Now take a specific product: the Apple iPhone. According to a paper published by the Asian Development Bank Institute in December 2010, data on bilateral trade are calculated assuming that the entire value of a traded good is created in the exporting country. If that ever made sense, it certainly does not in a global economy marked by increasingly complex supply chains. The iPhone was invented in America by Apple, an American company. The components are manufactured either inside or outside China by companies from several countries. The only part of the process that is unambiguously "Chinese" is the final assembly—a process the authors estimate contributes only $6.50 to the $178.96 wholesale value of an iPhone.[3]

Yet that entire $178.96 value ends up attributed to China in the calculation of trade statistics. As a result, the iPhone contributed nearly $1.6 billion to China's bilateral trade surplus with the United States in 2008 and nearly $2 billion in 2009. If the trade data had been used solely on the $6.50, the iPhone would have only added $34 million and $73 million respectively in those years to China's surplus. Just imagine when this type of situation is applied to all products being assembled in China and exported to the United States. According to an opinion piece titled "The $6.50 Trade War" in the *Wall Street Journal*, this Asian Development Bank Institute study should be required reading on Capitol Hill in Washington, D.C. It went on to say, "all of which illustrates the basic truth that trade has always benefited the American economy. Congress can't afford to forget that, no matter how much members would like to scapegoat Chinese factories for Washington's own policy mistakes."[4]

Of course, as the global supply chains become more and more complex, it is not possible for trade data to be absolutely accurate because companies supplying components may have their own mix of intellectual property development outside China. Thus it may be impossible to say precisely how much value China really adds. Nevertheless, the point to remember is that the reported U.S. trade imbalance with China is definitely overblown and misleading. U.S. lawmakers and the U.S. administration should consider this in making policy decisions.

A friend of mine who is involved in manufacturing technical products for export to Europe and America told me that chips for the iPhone come from suppliers such as South Korea's Samsung Group, Japan's Toshiba, and America's Intel and Broadcom. A German company, Infineon Technologies, supplies the chips that send and receive phone calls and data, while STMicroelectronics, an Italian- and French-owned company in Geneva, Switzerland, produces the gyroscope feature on the iPhone.

China tends to be merely the final stop in many a multinational's vast global production network. The most inexpensive link in this chain takes place in southern China, where workers are typically paid less than a dollar an hour to do the soldering, assembling, and packaging. If they didn't do it, would it create jobs in the United States? Probably not. Most American workers would never accept so low a wage and, in any event, in America that kind of assembly line work is typically done by machines.

Another overlooked detail is that by outsourcing components and hardware from China—matching low-cost Chinese suppliers with foreign companies that need products manufactured— American companies boost their return on capital. After joining the World Trade Organization in 2001, China's trade barriers dropped, creating opportunities for U.S. banks, insurance companies, and retailers. Also, China's rising demand for raw materials and commodities drives prices up, which is good news for the bottom lines of American steelmakers, mining firms, lumber companies, and other industrial giants. Not only that, cheap Chinese goods have helped to keep inflation low in the United States, thereby easing at least some of the burden of the recession.

It's All About Jobs

A study done by the National Retail Federation in the United States a few years ago concluded that imports from China have a net positive impact on U.S. employment. For every U.S. job lost to Chinese imports, eight jobs are created. And these jobs are in areas such as law, accounting, advertising, computer programming, and consultancies—all relatively high-paying professions. Erecting import tariffs against China, a move that anti-China advocates have suggested, would actually cost America jobs.

At the same time, we must not forget that China shares with the United States and other Western countries the need to create jobs for itself to keep its citizens happy. And in huge, populous China— which is still in many respects a developing nation with significant poverty, especially in rural areas—leaders know that job creation is especially necessary to maintain social stability and the credibility of one-party rule.

This could be a major reason why China is so reluctant to revalue its currency as abruptly as American politicians would like. If the value of the yuan was pegged to market forces, it might upset the country's carefully planned growth strategy, and a more expensive yuan would lead foreign companies to relocate to cheaper destinations. The fallout would include some Chinese factories being forced to close, leaving migrant workers jobless. Also, a more expensive yuan might lead to hyperinflation, creating even more instability and social unrest.

Many political observers thought President Barack Obama would be a more conciliatory leader than his predecessor. In August 2010, however, he made the following remarks at a fundraiser in Seattle for his fellow Democrat, Senator Patty Murray: "We did not become the most prosperous nation on Earth by rewarding greed and recklessness of the sort that helped cause the financial crisis . . . We did it by rewarding the values of hard work and responsibility. We did it by investing in the people who have built this country from the ground up: workers and families and small business owners and responsible entrepreneurs." All fine and good, but he went on to take a swipe at other countries who are actually *helping* the United States.

"We [became prosperous] because we out-worked and out-educated and out-competed other nations. That's who we are. That's what we need to be. Because right now, countries like China and India and South Korea and Germany, they are fighting as hard as they can for the jobs of the future . . . We are going to rebuild this economy stronger than it was before and at the heart of this rebuilding effort are three simple words: 'Made in America.' "[5]

But terms such as "Made in America" or "Assembled in China" are of little significance in the grand scheme of things. Today, products will be made from raw materials sourced wherever they can be found most inexpensively and put together wherever they can be most cheaply assembled and distributed. Today, China's economy is a hybrid, combining heavy government control in some sectors and a freewheeling capitalism that caters to foreign firms in others.

In the end, China's national interest is measured by results. As many Chinese leaders and spokespeople have said, China is not without faults—but nevertheless, in the end, "we have brought hundreds of millions of people out of poverty." Jeffrey Sachs, the distinguished Columbia University economist and author of *The End of Poverty*, said, "China is likely to be the first of the great poverty-stricken countries of the twentieth century to end poverty in the twenty-first century."[6] This achievement, and not the interests of the West, is what drives modern China.

Stephen Roach, a world-renowned economist, has been for several years chairman of Morgan Stanley Asia and resided in Hong Kong. He now splits his time between Asia and teaching at Yale University. In an opinion piece titled "The Silver Lining of Wage Increase," he said, "Notwithstanding all the hype over rising wages in China, it is entirely premature to declare an end to the global labor cost arbitrage that has long worked in China's favor. China remains highly competitive by international standards and the recent round of sharp increase in wages is not likely to alter that key conclusion . . . It is important to note that increasing worker compensation is a key ingredient of China's pro-consumption growth strategy . . . The global debates should focus more on the constructive implications of this important development for the long-awaited pro-consumption rebalancing of the Chinese economy."[7] Personal income in China currently amounts to about 40 percent of its GDP—still quite far below international standards.

Pressure from Below

One area of potential instability for China might come from the bottom up. In 2010, a rise in labor activism put pressure on the country's reputation as the low-cost "factory for the world." Shenzhen-based Foxconn Technology, which makes items for global corporations such as Apple, Dell, Hewlett-Packard, and Sony, was hit by labor unrest after a series of employee suicides. Foxconn, a division of Taiwan's Hon Hai Precision Industry Company, announced that it would be raising the basic salaries for many of its 800,000 workers. Meanwhile, four Honda Motor Company plants in Shenzhen were effectively shut down when employees went on strike demanding higher wages. Honda settled the strikes by agreeing to raises of 24–34 percent. Similar incidents happened at other factories, including a strike at the KOK Machinery factory in Kunshan, outside Shanghai, and a violent walkout at a Taiwan-funded rubber factory in eastern China's Jiangsu Province.

It is a delicate balance that China's leaders must find. On one hand, Beijing has backed some of the demands, encouraging local governments to raise the minimum wage. (Leading by example, the city of Beijing increased its minimum wage by 20 percent.) At a time when inflation has raised prices and an improving global economy has placed an even greater demand for China's factories to produce, Beijing wants to reduce a widening gap between the rich and poor and improve the lives of migrant workers. It is all part of China's goal to achieve *hexie shehui*, which translates as a "harmonious society."

But rising labor costs throughout the manufacturing sector would hurt small and medium-sized Chinese companies that are less able to absorb the increases than foreign-owned multinationals. And rising prices eventually mean that consumers around the world will pay more for a wide range of goods produced in China.

Meanwhile, as wages continue to rise in China's coastal regions, one solution Beijing is pursuing is a big push to "go West" in an effort to balance the country's further growth and development. China will also try to keep foreign investment in the country by providing incentives in the cities of the interior to lure both local and foreign firms. This strategy would have another benefit. Migrant workers, who numbered 211 million in 2009 and are expected to hit 350 million by 2050, would no longer have to work so far from home, placing less strain on the social fabric.

At the same time, efforts are being made to turn Shenzhen into more of a high-tech hub. Is that kind of shift possible? One of the factors attracting investment to China aside from cheap labor is the resilience that seems to be generic to the Chinese workforce, which is dominated by women. They are flexible and able to adapt quickly to changing circumstances. They can endure hardship and are quick learners. An absorbing account of their lives is well told in *Factory Girls: From Village to City in a Changing China*, by former *Wall Street Journal* China correspondent Leslie T. Chang.[8]

Mass migration of factories is, therefore, not likely in the near future because China's western hinterland can still offer diligent workers who are willing to work for a comparatively low wage. Government incentives will also encourage companies to stay in China. Some Chinese companies are beginning to expand abroad by acquiring companies in the West or setting up their own factories. Of course, these may initially involve higher-value products, but at least it will help create more jobs in America and Europe and help rebalance the overall global picture. Some of the Japanese auto companies, such as Toyota and Nissan, have already made this move.

For now, as China becomes more active in the higher technology and innovative sectors, it will still maintain its "factory of the world" status for some time to come. It will keep on assembling.

5

LAND OF MANY MARKETS

"THE MOUNTAINS ARE HIGH AND THE EMPEROR IS FAR AWAY"

When people talk about China's market of 1.3 billion consumers, they often imagine vast opportunities and wealth if they could simply reach all these potential buyers. But this broad-brush view is characteristic of those who do not understand China. I am reminded of a story I heard when I was the brand manager for a U.S. multinational in the early 1960s. Bata, a major shoe manufacturer, sent a sales executive to investigate the market potential of an emerging Latin American country. When the executive returned, he declared that very few people wore shoes in this region, so the potential to sell shoes was limited. To confirm these findings, the company sent a second executive to the same country. He came back with a report that very few people wore shoes, so there was *great* market potential.

Understanding China can be just as challenging, because it is not just one giant market to be exploited, nor will a one-size-fits-all approach work. China is seen as a culturally integrated, monolithic state with a one-party political system whose leaders issue unified directives to be followed throughout the country. This is far from the reality. Because of its size, China is really a set of loosely linked regional economies spread over a huge geographic area, making it all but impossible to enforce central directives. The old saying that opens the chapter—"The mountains are high and the emperor is far away"—is still relevant in the twenty-first century.

It is essential to get a sense of scale when one talks about the size of China. The People's Republic of China is the third-largest country in the world in terms of land mass, after Russia and Canada. It covers an area of nearly 4 million square miles, with eleven thousand miles of coastline. The top five of China's thirty-one provinces each has a population exceeding 75 million, and the list also includes several mega-cities—Beijing, Shanghai, Tianjin, and Chongqing (each with over 10 million people)—which are ranked as provinces because of their size and importance. Many Chinese provinces are larger than the largest European countries. For example, with a population of 87 million, Sichuan is larger than Germany, France, or Italy, not to mention the United Kingdom. It is challenging to imagine how a country this size can make any smooth transition.

North America is generally aware of the monumental shift that is under way in China. To take one example, by November 2009 China had replaced the United States as the largest auto manufacturer in the world, producing nearly 14 million vehicles, most of them passenger cars and vans. (And economists predict China's car market will grow tenfold by 2030.) Nearly 50 percent are local brands (Geely, Chery, BYD, Hafei), while the rest are joint ventures with foreign firms such as SAIC GM Wuling, Shanghai Volkswagen, Shanghai GM, FAW Volkswagen, Beijing Hyundai, Dongfeng Nissan, and FAW Toyota. Registered cars, buses, and trucks on the road were estimated to number well over 70 million in 2010.

The Chinese government has been encouraging car companies to consolidate and weaning them off their dependence on government subsidies and joint ventures with foreign companies. Shanghai Automotive Industry Corporation (SAIC), China FAW Group, Dongfeng Motors, and Zhongshan Automotive have been encouraged to buy out smaller competitors—an action similar to what happened in the steel industry. On the other hand, the government has also been spending considerable seed money to support auto-related ventures in many provinces—petrochemicals, steel, glassmaking, and rubber have all expanded to feed the automobile manufacturing sector. Increased car ownership has transformed sectors such as tourism and the development of shopping malls on the outskirts of major cities.

Until recently, China has avoided entering Europe or North America with its own automobile brands. With the standard of living rising for so many Chinese citizens, companies have been focusing on meeting demand from its massive home market first. But now, especially since China ranks among the most technologically advanced countries building electric cars, it is preparing to target Western markets. Geely's recent acquisition of Volvo is just the beginning. In addition to buying technology, China is buying global distribution.

Many Identities

Far from being a homogeneous market, China has a great deal of sociocultural diversity. It has fifty-six distinct ethnic groups, with Han Chinese being the predominant one (although even within the Han identity there are distinct linguistic and regional cultural traditions). The fifty-five remaining minorities maintain their own cultural traditions, customs, and dialects (although the written characters are similar across the country). In the southwestern province of Yunnan, for example, home to nearly half of China's ethnic groups, many citizens have more in common with their Burmese and Laotian neighbors than they do with the Han majority.

Within this framework, impending demographic shifts will become challenges for China to face—and important issues for the West to understand. The one-child policy of family planning (introduced in 1978), for example, was intended to alleviate social, economic, and environmental problems relating to overcrowding. But the result is a demographic shift toward an older, male-dominated population with too few young workers to support it.

Wang Feng, a demographer at the University of California, Irvine, suggests that by 2020, the 20–24-year-old demographic will be half of the 124 million of today, a shift that could affect competitiveness by driving up wages. During the same period, the proportion of the population over sixty will grow from today's 12 percent to 17 percent. This will create what is known in China as the "four-two-one" phenomenon: one adult child expected to provide support for two parents and four grandparents. If the average elderly individual's modest personal savings or pension ran out and state welfare failed, the elderly would be dependent on their very small families or neighbors for charity.[1]

Another shift is a surplus of males. In a society that has favored sons over daughters, the male-to-female ratio of births in China, as of 2009, was 122 to 100. (The global average is 107 to 100.) The gender imbalance will create a generation of men frustrated by their inability to find spouses, which could in turn lead to social problems and possibly the trafficking of girls and women from neighboring countries to be sold as brides. The imbalance may not be as severe as the official figures indicate because some newborn girls may not have been reported by their parents to the local registries, especially in the rural areas.

In McKinsey & Company's 2009 Annual Chinese Consumer Study, "One Country, Many Markets," the authors suggest there is no such thing as a "one China strategy."[2] The southern cities of Guangzhou and Shenzhen, located a three-hour car drive apart in the province of Guangdong, are among the wealthiest in China. Both have a population the size of a small European nation and produce low-cost exports for the global market. Yet they are as different in demographic profile, language, and consumer preferences as France is from Germany. The majority of Shenzhen's citizens are young migrant workers who speak Mandarin to communicate across local dialects. At night, just like young people everywhere, they like to congregate in local bars. In Guangzhou, the population is older, with only about 25 percent migrants. They primarily speak Cantonese and frequent restaurants to drink and dine with family members.

Few in the West understand these kinds of distinctions. Although the United States is a mixture of many ethnic groups and cultures, the rise of mass media, beginning in the early days of radio and television, has created a relatively homogeneous consumer market. In America, for example, companies can do a national roll-out after conducting test marketing in a center such as Kansas City. If "boyfriend jeans" or patchwork scarves are in style, the trend will probably spread quickly across the country.

In China, this may only happen within the country's largest urban centers. In these cities, the Internet has the greatest impact, and foreign multinationals such as Dell, McDonald's, and Yum Group (the Kentucky-based firm that includes KFC and Pizza Hut) have expanded their operations. China represents the biggest opportunity for every consumer company, so these and other multinationals are busy expanding throughout the country. As Internet use penetrates rural areas, there may be more opportunities to create national campaigns. But evidence that China is a land of many markets can easily be seen in the way even multinationals must cater to local preferences.

For McDonald's, that means a quarter of the menu must reflect regional tastes, which includes Kalubi beef or spicy chicken on a fried rice patty glazed with soy sauce, along with red bean paste ice-cream sundaes. KFC offers many special items—including Chinese favorites such as shredded pork soup, *youtiao* (fried dough), and preserved egg porridge. Early in 2010 the Chinese arm of Kraft Foods even launched a whole wheat biscuit line in three flavors: Chinese red date, black sesame seed, and peanut. (According to Chinese herbology, red dates boost energy and clean blood, while black sesame seeds and peanuts are good for the kidneys.) PepsiCo Foods (China) has created potato chip flavors that include grilled mushroom, Peking duck, and Sichuan spice. As for Danone, that company produces yogurt with seven different levels of sweetness for sale in different regions.

There are other signs of a shift in the marketing focus, especially by multinational corporations. Faye Xia is the manager of marketing and consumer insights for greater China at U.S.-based International Flavors & Fragrances (IFF), one of the world's top flavor and fragrance producers. She says in a recent report that companies must take into account the different regional tastes in China. "Usually people in the north prefer food to be salty, but people who live in the south prefer food to be fresh. In the East, people have more preference for sweet taste while spicy foods are popular in inland China."[3]

This is probably why Procter & Gamble decided to establish an Innovation Center in Beijing—a sparkling $70 million home for the company's regional R&D efforts—to research, source, and develop products for China and the rest of Asia without having to rely on its headquarters in Cincinnati. A simulated Chinese home in this center enables researchers to observe consumers as they wash their hair, brush their teeth, and change their baby's diaper, then make immediate prototypes. In the past, products were all invented in the United States and pushed out to markets around the world in a command-and-control fashion. In the future, it is likely that some of the new products may be developed in Beijing for various business units to market especially in emerging markets. In *Fortune* magazine, Robert McDonald, CEO and chairman of Procter & Gamble, was quoted as saying, "You have to discreetly innovate for every one of those consumers on that economic curve and if you don't do that, you'll fail." That includes the "$2 a day" consumers in China.[4]

Fanning Out Across China

Most multinationals have elected to focus their strategic expansion only on China's top-tier cities, where wealth and buying power are most concentrated. The rationale seems reasonable. If even a small percentage of these markets can be secured, this could translate into substantial revenues in absolute dollars compared to other markets around the world. But one of many shifts taking place within China will challenge this approach. As prices and cost of living soar in the big metropolitan centers, more and more young, educated, and experienced professionals are choosing to move to second-tier cities. (Just as the same socioeconomic group in the United States migrated from big cities to suburbs.) Cities considered to have the best living conditions include Qingdao in Shandong Province, Suzhou and Taizhou in Jiangsu Province, Fuzhou in Fujian Province, and Ningbo in Zhejiang Province.

According to a recent survey conducted by insurance giant Manulife-Sinochem, there are four reasons for relocating: more affordable housing, the lower cost of educating children, less traffic congestion, and cleaner air. This phenomenon is driven by corporations that move to emerging second-tier cities to escape the high costs and fierce competition in major centers and then create a demand for managerial talent. Young professionals then find themselves moving up the corporate ladder when they relocate.

Meanwhile, this migration of workers also ties into the central government's push to balance progress geographically.[5]

On a global scale, these trends are closely related to a marketing shift that represents new challenges for Western companies. According to *The Keys to the Kingdom: Unlocking China's Consumer Power*, a report produced by the Boston Consulting Group, a company doing business five years ago in seventy locations could reach 70 percent of consumers in the middle and affluent classes. To achieve that coverage today, it would need to be in more than three times that many locations. The spread of consumer spending power across China means that companies must constantly expand their geographical footprint. At the same time, the vast scale makes it vital to cluster cleverly in the most appropriate locations in order to guarantee long-term growth.[6]

To understand the vast market in China, the first thing to consider is the major urban centers. A 2008 study by McKinsey & Company, "Meeting the Challenges of China's Growing Cities," predicts that by 2025 China will have at least eight megacities the likes of which the world has never seen. These cities—Beijing, Shanghai, Chengdu, Chongqing, Guangzhou, Shenzhen, Tianjin, and Wuhan—will each have populations of well over 10 million people. And Chongqing is outstripping all the rest; it is close to being the first city with a population of 30 million.[7]

Late in 2010, *Fortune* magazine cited a survey result of the fifth annual Emerging Business Cities, where 1,278 Chinese senior managers were asked to rank fifty selected cities based on overall business environment, cost of doing business, local talent pool, and quality of life. The following five cities were selected as potentially the next generation of megacities: Suzhou, Qingdao, Shenzhen, Ningbo, and Dalian.[8]

But China is likely to follow a different model to urbanization than that of Western countries. In the West, cities grew as a result of industrialization: people migrated from rural areas to cities to work in factories. In China, factories will remain in rural areas (where land and labor are cheap), and the growth of megacities will be related to their role as service centers rather than hotbeds of manufacturing employment. But what lures individuals to cities will always be the same: the chance to achieve a higher standard of living. That's why it is a priority for the central government to develop infrastructure links between these megacities and the smaller centers in the surrounding region.

In recent years, China has been investing heavily in highways and rail networks as the country begins to knit the regions together. These shifts in infrastructure are also part of a government strategy to push development and investment toward the western hinterlands, where poverty is still widespread. The planned Chinese high-speed rail network will be the largest in the world. This should effectively shrink what has been a geographically immense country and, in theory, lay the foundation for a national market.

But there are impediments. The mountains are still high, and the emperor is still far away. That philosophy has bred a great deal of autonomy, so trade between cities and provinces can best be characterized as fiercely competitive rather than cooperative, preventing the formation of a single market. Hence the need for Western businesses to continue to the "many markets" model.

In November 2010, the Boston Consulting Group published *Big Prizes in Small Places: China's Rapidly Multiplying Pockets of Growth*. Here are some of the salient points:

- Middle-income and affluent consumers (MAC) residing in China's smaller cities offer an unprecedented opportunity for companies looking for growth. Willingness to spend and trade up is significantly greater in small cities than in the major cities.

- MAC population will increase to more than 400 million over the next decade, and two-thirds will reside in second- and third-tier cities.

- Today, to reach 80 percent of the MAC population, a company must be in 340 urban locations. To achieve the same coverage in ten years, a company will need to be in 550 urban centers.

- Consumers in small cities enjoy lower cost of living, so they have greater purchasing power and are more willing to spend.

- Companies should not assume that their big-city business models will work equally well in smaller cities, where spending behaviors, product preferences, and outreach channels may be different.

Life in the Regions

It is also necessary to understand the regional nature of this immense country. In addition to the Pearl River Delta (which includes cities such as Hong Kong, Macao, Guangzhou, and Shenzhen) and the Greater Shanghai area, both of which have long been economic forces, there are a number of zones, belts, and regions that will be additional powerhouses driving China's national economy in the future. In the following pages, I offer my observations on the shifting economic geography of modern China.

The Chengdu-Chongqing Economic Zone includes Chengdu, the capital city of Sichuan Province in China's southwest region, and Chongqing, where China's first bonded inland port is being built. The latter is China's largest city in terms of population and land area (Shanghai still leads in urban population). The National Development and Reform Commission, a macroeconomic management agency under the Chinese State Council, has drafted plans to include fifteen cities in Sichuan Province and thirty-one districts and counties in Chongqing, covering an area of about 124,000 square miles. With a high-speed rail link soon to be completed, citizens of Chengdu can be eating hotpot in Chongqing in fifty-six minutes. This "one hour circle" is part of the overall plan to develop the zone. Not surprisingly, all these changes have attracted Western businesses. In 2009, Intel moved its manufacturing and testing plants from Shanghai to Chongqing. Meanwhile, Hewlett-Packard has built a manufacturing base in Chongqing to assemble 40 million laptops annually, with production capacity reportedly planned to reach 80 million.

Located in Anhui Province, the Wanjiang River Urban Belt is the first—and so far only—area that has been approved by the central government as a national-level industrial transfer demonstration zone. It has been given priority to "act first and try first" by positioning itself as a base for advanced manufacturing and services. Located not far from Shanghai and offering many cost advantages, the area is a good choice for companies in the Yangtze River Delta area that wish to expand. Raw materials, equipment manufacturing, textiles, high technology, up-to-date agricultural techniques, and modern services are highlighted as the six pillar industries. This zone includes two counties and nine cities, the largest being Hefei and Wuhu.

Designated as an important free trade area for regional economic cooperation with the Association of Southeast Asian Nations (ASEAN) countries, the Beibu Gulf Economic Zone is in the Guangxi Zhuang autonomous region, west of the Pearl River Delta and just north of Hainan Island. It covers an area of about 26,408 square miles, with a population of more than 12 million spread out over six cities: Nanning, Beihai, Qinzhou, Fangchenggang, Chongzuo, and Yulin. This state-approved zone will be a trading hub with ASEAN countries, particularly Vietnam, Laos, Thailand, and Myanmar.

One of the most strategically located shifts is taking place in the western Taiwan Straits Economic Zone. This area, falling within Fujian Province, lies opposite Taiwan and is intended to forge a stronger political and economic relationship across the Taiwan Straits. The Fujian government also wanted to become more competitive with other economic zones, such as the Yangtze River Delta (Shanghai) to the north and Pearl River Delta (Hong Kong) to the south. One of its advantages is that it shares ancestral origins, dialects, culture, and traditions with Taiwan.

One area that is certain to attract international attention is the Tibet Autonomous Region. This area, which represents about half of ethno-cultural Tibet, was traditionally dependent on farming and herding. In January 2010, the central government announced plans to achieve "leapfrog development" in Tibet. The plan aims to build the region into a "strategic reserve of natural resources," further reducing the poverty of the Tibetan people. Tibet has more than three thousand proven mineral reserves and China's largest chromium and copper deposits. Mineral resources will contribute close to 30 percent of the regional GDP in the next ten years. Tourism will continue to play a significant part in the economy.

Literally translating as "new frontier," Xingjiang is a northwestern region that is China's largest administrative district at nearly a million square miles. The Xinjiang Uygur Autonomous Region has abundant oil reserves as well as the largest natural gas producing area in the country, both of which feed the eastern coastal region's economic growth. It is known for its "one black, one white, and one red" industrial chain, referring to oil, cotton, and tomatoes. There are plans for increased financial support from the central government and investments from state-owned companies to develop resources such as petrochemicals, coal, nonferrous metals, and agriculture. Rising tourism will also contribute to this region's economy.

In addition to these zones, belts, and regions, there are thirty-one provinces in China. Four of these provinces are actually cities that have been elevated to provincial status and report directly to the central government. Here are the ten largest provinces, which, combined with the major city-centers of Beijing, Shanghai, Chongqing, and Tianjin, represent more than 800 million people:

- Henan
- Shandong
- Sichuan
- Guangdong
- Jiangsu
- Hebei
- Hunan
- Anhui
- Hubei
- Zhejiang.

Henan (River South), with a population of 95 million, is one of China's "breadbaskets," producing wheat, beef, and oil-bearing crops, with the largest herds of cattle and buffalo in the nation. Coal, oil, gold, and natural gas play major roles in this region's economy. The massive, $3.5 billion Xiaolangdi dam project on the Yellow River produces 5.1 billion kilowatt hour (kWh) of electricity annually. Multinationals such as Nokia, Toray Engineering, Mitsubishi, McDonald's, and General Electric are active in this province.

Shandong (East of the Mountains), with a population of 90 million, is home to China's biggest gold reserves, as well as the nation's second-largest deposits of diamonds, copper, and oil.

Both Tsingtao, China's largest brewery, and the now world-famous appliance maker Qingdao Haier have located their operations in this province. Huaneng Power International Holdings is Asia's largest independent power company. Canadian firms Bombardier and Power Corporation of Canada have a joint venture with China National Railway Locomotive and Rolling Stock to make passenger rail cars near Qingdao.

The province of Sichuan is similar in size, with 87 million people. It is the country's largest gas-producing region, with extensive carbon-based energy resources, and it produces China's highest hydropower generation. (One of the World Bank's largest financing packages was used to build a massive hydroelectric plant in this province.) Companies such as General Electric, Ericsson, Siemens, Alcatel, Lafarge, Bayer, and Coca-Cola, and banks such as HSBC, Standard Chartered, and BNP are all active in the province.

With Hong Kong as the main gateway to China, especially in the 1970s and '80s, the province of Guangdong received most of China's early foreign investment. The economic zone of Shenzhen has become the major export processing center for consumer products destined for America and Europe. Many Hong Kong- and Taiwan-based companies moved across the border to take advantage of cheaper labor and land. Multinationals did the same. Products such as textiles, packaged foods, toys, electrical appliances, televisions, and cameras are assembled here. It is the world's capital for OEM companies—manufacturers who produce products for brand owners (both local and international). Multinationals such as Procter & Gamble, Avon, PepsiCo, ICI, Amway, Motorola, Nokia, and General Electric all have a presence here. With a great deal of infrastructure being constructed (or planned) linking Hong Kong and Macao with cities in this province, the Pearl River Delta is the powerhouse of the future.

Reputed to be China's most densely populated province with 78 million inhabitants, Jiangsu is the third-largest provincial economy (after Guangdong and Shandong), boasting a well-balanced industrial structure. The belt between Nanjing and Shanghai is considered one of the most dynamic parts of the Yangtze River Delta region. Neighboring Shanghai has the same stimulating effect on this province as Hong Kong has on Guangdong. Nanjing reportedly has the highest Internet usage in the country. Multinationals such as Motorola, Ericsson, Nokia, Sharp, Siemens, Kimberly-Clark, PepsiCo, Ford, and Upjohn are all active here. The Singapore government and Singapore-based companies play an active role in this province. Famous as the capital of six dynasties, Nanjing is a leading tourist destination. The ancient cities of Suzhou ("the Venice of China") and Wuxi (the "pearl of Lake Tai") are major attractions for visitors.

Along with the Pearl River Delta in the south and the Yangtze River Delta in the central part of the country, Hebei (River North) is the third key component of a coastal development initiative promoted by the central government. Encircling Beijing and Tianjin, Hebei enjoys spill-over benefits from its neighboring economic giants. Boasting important power plants and oil fields, it is an important supplier of coal, petroleum, and iron. Multinationals with operations in this province of 70 million people include Siemens, Hoechst, Toyota, Mitsubishi, DuPont, Ingersoll, Phillips, and Unilever.

Hunan (population 68 million) is called "Lake South" because it borders the second-largest body of water in China: Dongting Lake. With its large deposits of antimony and tungsten (among the largest in the world), the province is a major producer of nonferrous metals, as well as lead, zinc, mercury, and graphite. Capitalizing on its location between the Yangtze River Delta to the north and Guangdong Province to the south, Hunan is building an industrial corridor along the Beijing-Guangzhou rail artery. Siemens, together with a local partner in this province, is developing a prototype for a Chinese bullet train. And on a cultural-historical note, Chairman Mao's birthplace—the village of Shaoshan—is located in this province.

Bordering Jiangsu, and often regarded as the poor cousin to the more prosperous province, is Anhui, with a population of 65 million. Traditionally seen as the source of cheap migrant workers, Anhui still has a fairly wide industrial base in metallurgy, petrochemicals, building materials, coal, and food processing. It is also known for companies producing refrigerators, air conditioners, and washing machines as well as household cleaning goods. Leading foreign investors are mostly Japanese companies such as Sanyo, Hitachi, Fujitsu, Toyota, and Mitsubishi. Unilever, BP Amoco, and Siemens also have investments here.

Hubei (Lake North), with a population of 62 million, is home to the controversial Three Gorges Dam project. This province's capital, Wuhan, is also one of the most developed cities in central China. Located in the heart of a rich agricultural region, it is a leading rice producer and is also known for wheat, cotton, and oil-bearing crops. Considerable foreign and local investment has been directed into telecommunications and utilities. Multinationals active in Hubei also include General Motors, Coca-Cola, Hyundai, and Pilkington Glass. The French car manufacturer Citroen is part of the Dongfeng Motors joint venture.

With a population of 48 million, the province of Zhejiang is comparatively smaller but not less vigorous. Known for its silk products, the capital city, Hangzhou, is the largest textile distribution center in Asia, especially known for its chemical fibers. Pharmaceuticals is the other key industry, with substantial investment from foreign pharma multinationals. In fact, more than 250 pharmaceutical enterprises make their home in this province. Zhejiang is a favorite destination for Taiwan investors, partly because Ningbo, its deepwater port, is such an important natural asset.

Coping With Diversity

Given the historical self-interest in the various regions, and despite the central government's best efforts, the shift to one national market will likely take at least a decade, if it happens at all. That doesn't mean China's influence as an economic power—both at home and abroad—will be any less dramatic. It simply means China is a more complicated market to move into than some foreign enterprises might imagine. And, internally, it will require a different kind of national model as an economic generator.

Different products and services require different business models and approaches to marketing. Furthermore, because provinces and municipalities compete against each other for foreign investments, multinationals will need to cater to certain local rules and regulations. For example, companies may have to set up separate legal entities for each province or even big cities.

What companies need to keep in mind is that China is not one market in which a single, short-term approach will be successful. It is wiser to focus first on a city-by-city approach (or province-by-province, or region-by-region). In the West, achieving a large market share is a common goal. In China, if you were able to secure 1 percent of the market, the absolute numbers would still be huge. By all means keep the international branding and image, but allow some flexibility in product offering. The high-tech sector and other big-ticket items such as aircraft manufacturing would need very different strategies, for example, in part because of the political issues in play in China, as well as regulatory differences in the various regions.

Finally, should the head of China operations report to an Asia-Pacific president? My view is that because of the size and complexity and its exceptional potential, multinationals should consider operating China as a separate entity reporting directly to the CEO. Head offices need to allow flexibility to the Chinese management. Avoid making judgments and developing plans based on the Western way of looking at things.

Even today, with all the progress in automobile, rail, and air travel as well as the uniting effect of telecommunications, especially the Internet, China remains a land of many markets, one in which regional strategies are more important than national ones.

6

GUANXI AND *MIANZI*

In America, as in most of the Western world, money and power dominate the business and political landscape. Money and power are important drivers in China too. But what Westerners often misunderstand is the special significance and profoundly complex character of relationships, reputation, honor, and prestige in Chinese culture. These are represented by the twin concepts of *guanxi*, referring to relationships, connections, and reciprocal obligations, and *mianzi*, which means "face" or "reputation." While chasing money and power may be common in both East and West, it is impossible to understand how that race is run in China without understanding *guanxi* and *mianzi*.

The Ties That Bind

In almost anything you may read about Chinese culture, *guanxi* is mentioned. I know from my experience living and working in America that the Western equivalent—an individual's networks of colleagues and acquaintances—is relatively impersonal and most often associated with business dealings. In China, however, the significance of *guanxi* runs deep, permeating every aspect of a person's life. Sometimes it is mistakenly thought to be analogous to corruption. Yes, China is still improving its legal system, which does not yet match internationally recognized standards. But corruption plays no greater part in *guanxi* than it does in human relations in the West.

The Chinese character *guan* means a gate or barrier and *xi* means a link, or a relationship. So the word literally refers to passing a barrier and getting connected. In popular usage, it refers to a relationship formed between a person who has done someone a favor and the person who received the favor and is expected to reciprocate in the future. So the meaning of *guanxi* includes all forms of relationships at all levels of society. In that way, it's much broader than the Western notion of networking.

Forging connections relating to business dealings is universal; *guanxi* is similar to what Westerners often describe as *pull*, referring to a web of contacts that may help you get things done more quickly, efficiently, or cheaply. While bribes may not be involved, it is true that in some cases the official who helps you navigate through a government bureaucracy or consummate a deal may one day ask you to use your connections to help them get their child into a competitive college or university. The art of giving gifts during festive seasons, especially at Chinese New Year, is one that must be acquired. But this can be true in the West, as well. In essence, lobbyists in Washington are basically *guanxi* agents on behalf of their corporate interests.

The global financial crisis of 2008 and 2009 resulted in the closing of as many as sixty-seven thousand factories in China because of the slowdown in exports. It especially affected small factories that were already suffering from a combination of rising labor, transportation, and raw material costs, as well as the appreciating yuan. When some workers began protesting over lost back wages, there was fear that the result would be an explosion of unrest. Yet China experienced relatively few problems among the groups most affected: unemployed workers and university graduates unable to get their first jobs. This is largely because of the close-knit structure of Chinese families, which is an extension of *guanxi*.

Even though I have spent a great deal of time in America, I am still surprised by the number of homeless people I see on the streets of cities such as New York, Los Angeles, and San Francisco. In China, joblessness seldom translates into homelessness or destitution. Those who lose their jobs can almost always rely on family support to get them through a difficult period. At least they will have a roof over their heads and will not starve. That is why the central government mounted a 4 trillion yuan ($586 billion) stimulus package to help generate domestic consumption so factories could reopen and people would be rehired. Stability and social harmony are always on top of the central government's agenda, and the family *guanxi* is a key element in maintaining stability through economic hardship.

Guanxi is also related to trust. While the West strains under the weight of its legal system, a handshake is far more important than a contract in China. This is a major area of frustration for Chinese businesspeople in their dealings with counterparts in the West. To the Chinese, if one side or the other needs to pull out the contract and refer to certain clauses, the relationship is already in deep trouble. If genuine *guanxi* exists, both sides trust each other and there is no need for legal documents.

This is not dissimilar to the concept of microcredit, which has its origin in the Grameen Bank in Bangladesh. This community development organization was founded by Muhammad Yunus, who was subsequently awarded a Nobel Prize in 2006. Microcredit is based on trust. Small loans are given without collateral to those who cannot meet even the most minimal qualifications to gain access to traditional credit. Of course, in today's highly legalistic environment, the handshake tradition would, at best, be limited only to some Chinese-to-Chinese dealings.

American executives operating in China should cultivate *guanxi* themselves, not simply leave it to local Chinese colleagues or partners. Beware, though, not to fall too deeply into the *guangxiwang*, or network. For example, local contacts might believe that as an American you can influence the American Embassy to obtain visas or help their children gain admission to prestigious U.S. universities. Does this mean *guanxi* is for sale? In some cases, I suppose it is, in the same way that the lobbying profession in America could be described as *guanxi* for sale. But it is such an ingrained cultural habit in China that few would see it that way. (Unlike Americans, the Chinese do not often distinguish between the professional and the personal. If things become uncomfortable, the foreigner's best approach is to politely explain the difference.)

Here is another example of how *guanxi* works. In the early
1990s, when I was chairman of Hong Kong–based Inchcape Pacific,
I chose to set up our first office in mainland China in Nanjing, one
of the country's most important business centers. I began visiting
the city to cultivate my *guanxi* with municipal officials, including the
party secretary, who is the highest-ranking Communist Party official in any region, and the mayor. At first, the meetings were very
formal, with all parties sitting on traditional armchairs and their
respective entourages facing each other in a row.

Then, when I was returning to Hong Kong from Los Angeles
one day, I boarded a flight and coincidentally found myself sitting next to Nanjing's party secretary. It is unlikely I would have
spent such an intimate and prolonged period of time with him in
any other circumstance. Because the Chinese culture leads people
to believe strongly in fate, by the end of our fourteen-hour flight
the party secretary felt that our chance meeting meant we were
destined to become friends. When we parted, he said I should let
him know if there was ever any assistance he could offer. Fate, of
course, helps, but the key is in the follow-through.

On my next visit to Nanjing, the party secretary sent two
members of his staff to pick me up at the airport. I handed my
passport to one of them, who then handled the immigration pro-
cedure on my behalf. When we left the airport a police car with
its lights flashing acted as our security escort. On another visit,
my wife, Janet, was with me, and the party secretary insisted on
personally taking us on a tour of the city—despite being the most
senior official in the government hierarchy.

Through this *guanxi*, I also became close friends with the mayor
of Nanjing. At that time, major cities in China were eagerly competing for foreign investment, especially among Chinese business
people in Hong Kong and Southeast Asia. When the mayor visited Hong Kong to promote his city, I organized a luncheon in
his honor. One of the guests pointed out to the mayor that those
who attended the lunch accounted for about 60 percent of Hong
Kong's stock market capitalization. Eventually a couple of them
made investments in Nanjing. This act of reciprocity went a long
way toward cementing the *guanxi*.

I wanted to set up an import-export office of Inchcape Pacific in Nanjing, but in those days China prohibited foreign businesses from trading in the local currency. I approached the party secretary for help and he asked the mayor to grant Inchcape the first-ever trading license in local currency. If Beijing questioned it, he proposed that it be described as a test, a pilot project that, if successful, could be good for the country because it opened Chinese business up to the world. No doubt someone would have been fortunate enough to get this first license in Nanjing but, because of the *guanxi* I had established, it turned out to be Inchcape Pacific. We were the distributor representing many Western multinationals in consumer and industrial products at that time, and many of them benefited from this beachhead in China.

When our competitors in Hong Kong heard about it, they thought I must have bribed the officials. But in all the times I met with the party secretary or the mayor in my hotel suite, bribery never came up. In 1992, I was made an honorary citizen of Nanjing as well as an economic adviser to the city. All of this came about because I was able to take advantage of *guanxi*—a relationship built upon a foundation of friendship, trust, and respect.

Another example was when the movie *Seven Days in Tibet* was produced by Columbia Pictures (which had been acquired by Sony Corporation some years back). Beijing asked the (then) CEO of Sony, Idei-san (Nobuyuki Idei), to stop the distribution. Sony tried to explain that it could not do that sort of thing in America, but to no avail. In the minds of the Chinese leadership, when you own something outright (i.e., 100 percent) you normally should be in total control. Sony was now concerned that this episode might affect its extensive investments in China. I took on a consulting assignment to help with the impasse.

While I used my channels of contact to help further explain the matter, I also made two recommendations. First, Sony should do something to demonstrate its commitment to help promote technological education in China. In this regard, Sony signed an agreement with the Exploratorium in San Francisco to establish a technical exhibition in Beijing. The Minister of Education officiated at the opening, with widespread publicity. The second recommendation was that Sony should start cultivating relationships with second- and third-tier officials and invite them to Japan. Some of these officials will become ministers and will remember that Sony treated them with respect when they were in their more junior roles—thus establishing *guanxi* in a long-term relationship and giving these officials a lot of *mianzi*.

Reciprocal Dignity

And, like one member of a set of twins, *guanxi* is a concept that is inextricably tied to *mianzi*. I gave the officials face when they came to Hong Kong, and they reciprocated when I needed their help in Nanjing. The same would apply in the case of Sony and its tie to the movie company.

Mianzi translates as "face," and it refers to an individual's prestige, status, self-respect, and honor. Similar to the Western idea of dignity, *mianzi* is the basis for social standing and reputation. In the West, to "lose face"—for example, to have made a mistake that makes colleagues or friends respect you a little less, at least temporarily—is merely embarrassing and unpleasant. But in the Chinese culture, where it is said that a person needs face the way a tree needs bark, it is amplified to the point of being profoundly, and even paralyzingly, humiliating. The social order is based on knowing appropriate behavior based on one's social status and relationship to others. As a result, causing someone to "lose face" may result in irreparable damage to an individual's *guanxi*, affecting everything from social relations to business dealings.

Knowing how serious some violations of *mianzi* can be, I have watched in horror as inexperienced Western executives, taught to speak their minds and act boldly and decisively, lose their cool during negotiations and demonstrate it by raising their voices or storming out of meetings. In Chinese business or political relations, this can be disastrous. In China, one needs to show patience. As I've said, "Everything is possible but nothing is easy." This is what I always advise my Western colleagues and friends. Always be polite and respectful.

I also remember admiring an experienced American businessman who understood the Chinese mentality. He was asked during the final negotiations of a deal to lower his bid. Instead of protesting a change like this at so late a date, he made a counterproposal: that the final price would include the training of Chinese staff in the United States. Of course, training was critical to the long-term success of the project, but by offering it when he did, he helped his Chinese counterpart save face in the eyes of his superiors by extracting something extra from the American. He knew that treating business as a Western-style competition, where the most powerful opponent wins, is counterproductive when negotiating in China.

Many Western executives and political officials complain that their Chinese colleagues tend not to speak their minds at meetings, especially when the meeting involves a sizable number of people. This is because they do not want to lose face by saying something wrong or making a poor proposal that is rejected. By contrast, in the West people are taught that speaking up, even if your ideas are mundane or you have nothing new to add, is important to demonstrate that you are an active participant who has provided some input.

In the West, emphasis is on personal achievement, creativity, competition, initiative, and independence. In China, young people are taught not to question but to accept authority—from parents, grandparents, and superiors in a workplace. Everything is consensus driven, and people are expected to fall in line. This extends to the common practice of government officials referring to themselves not by their names but by the bureau (or *danwei*) they represent.

When I was getting my MBA at Wharton, there was an event just before graduation involving a group of four students who sat facing four professors for a two-hour session. This was back in 1961. We were asked a broad range of questions that touched on everything from business principles to current affairs to social and cultural issues. Often, a professor would ask one of us to comment on what a classmate had just said. As a young man raised in China and Hong Kong, I found the experience extremely stressful. If a classmate offered what I considered to be an incorrect answer, should I point this out, making me look good at the expense of my classmate's loss of face? In the West, I was learning how people debate and even argue quite vociferously, without it becoming personal. Afterwards, friendships are usually unaffected. Not only would this kind of behavior be viewed as terribly rude in China, it would be considered a serious violation of *mianzi*.

Knowing this, Western multinationals should be cautious when conducting market research, because one characteristic of *mianzi* is the "soft no." Unlike in the West, communication in China is indirect, implicit, coded in the context of a conversation. People understand intuitively what is really being said, whereas Westerners would interpret the message literally (and often incorrectly). So, when asked direct questions, consumers are unlikely to say what they really think for fear of giving a "wrong answer" or offending. They may say what they think researchers want to hear, assuming, as is usually the case when dealing with fellow Chinese citizens, that the true meaning will be understood.

Similarly, if a Western businessperson conducts a reference check and hears "I really did not know that person very well," or any similarly neutral but ambiguous response, it is a clear signal to look much more closely at a candidate who may have serious liabilities.

This reminds me of the time when I was seeking reelection to the Hong Kong Legislature. If someone I approached to support me said they knew what to do, this would normally be a "soft no" to avoid making me lose face. But if they said "Mingxun [or Paul (my English name)], I will definitely vote for you"—then the chance of my getting their support would be high.

Violations of *mianzi* can also lead to retaliation. If an expatriate manager, wittingly or unwittingly, causes a Chinese official to lose face, he may discover the next day that his factory is having difficulty getting water or electricity. Understanding *mianzi* might even lead to more productive results in political affairs as well. In January 2009, shortly before he was confirmed as Barack Obama's secretary of the treasury, Timothy Geithner publicly declared that "President Obama, backed by the conclusions of a broad range of economists, believes that China is manipulating its currency." At a time when China was trying hard to establish itself as a legitimate and honorable player in the international arena, even the implication that the country was intentionally trying to gain an unfair trade advantage would be seen as a powerful insult.

Dictating to China what it should do with its currency causes the Chinese to lose face to America and the international community. Publicly, of course, the reaction was expressed in a formal manner. Responding to Geithner, Hua Ercheng, chief economist at China Construction Bank, said: "I was very disappointed and surprised at the remarks. We are concerned about rising trade protectionism in the U.S."

But Nicholas Lardy, an economist who specializes in China at the Peterson Institute for International Economics in Washington, recognized the faux pas. Chinese officials "will be more than annoyed," he said. "They don't like being singled out, and they don't like countries explicitly criticizing them for the way they run their economy."[1]

Similarly, I always advise my friends in Washington, D.C., that if the U.S. government has concerns about China's valuation of its currency, a more practical approach would be to avoid conflict by quietly sending officials to China for low-key discussions—preferably out of the glare of the mass media—with their Chinese counterparts. Rather than being excessively concerned with using power and influence to force China to comply with its wishes, it is more effective to manage the process so it appears that China made its own decision. This is the art of "giving face."

Other recent events also demonstrate my point. Whenever the United States sells arms to Taiwan or welcomes the Dalai Lama to Washington, a similar chain reaction occurs. What in the West is seen as politics-as-usual is regarded in China as another case of the country losing face internationally. Chinese responses, which may be even more irritated than usual, reflect this concern.

About the Taiwan arms deal, China's foreign minister, Yang Jiechi, said that the United States should "truly respect China's core interests and major concerns and immediately rescind the mistaken decision to sell arms to Taiwan . . . to avoid damaging broader China-U.S. relations." And commenting on Washington's decision to host a visit by the Dalai Lama, Zhu Weiqun, a vice minister of the United Front Work Department of China's Communist Party, said that meeting with the Dalai Lama "would damage trust and cooperation between our two countries."

Understanding the nuances of these key twin concepts of *guanxi* and *mianzi,* and especially the idea of "giving others face," is essential for anyone from the West who might be involved in business or politics in China. It is an extraordinary country, with complexities and subtleties that need to be carefully navigated by world travelers.

7

SOFT POWER

WINNING HEARTS AND MINDS

In my earlier career as a regional manager of multinational corporations, I used to travel extensively throughout Asia, including, of course, China. Wherever I went, I always reserved an afternoon or an evening for one of my personal interests. I would visit areas where antiques and indigenous arts and crafts were sold so I could add a few items to my collection. I came to admire the craftsmanship that existed in various periods of Chinese history, reflecting a highly sophisticated civilization. Historically, China was a major power in East Asia. The recent transformation of its image and influence should, therefore, be viewed more as a Chinese renaissance. And, as part of a momentous shift in international dynamics, it is being exported to the world through the use of *soft power*.

Soft power is the key strategy of China's leaders as they guide the country's emergence as a global superpower. The three goals of soft power are to create a more positive perception of China in the eyes of the international community (which means countering the view that it poses a potential threat); to help people understand the social, economic, and political realities of the modern Chinese state; and to build acceptance of its rise to power.

The contemporary use of the term originated in 1990, when it was coined by Harvard scholar Joseph Nye, although he articulated it in more detail in 2004, in *Soft Power: The Means to Success in World Politics*. Writing in the context of America, he referred to soft power as "the ability to get what you want through attraction rather than coercion or payments. It arises from the attractiveness of a country's culture, political ideals, and policies. When our policies are seen as legitimate in the eyes of others, our soft power is enhanced."[1]

In Nye's original definition, soft power included neither foreign investment and aid nor formal diplomatic efforts. Today, the term is generally used by politicians and international affairs experts to refer to achieving influence abroad and enhancing a country's image through persuasion and presenting appealing values that others will want to emulate. It involves everything from cultural and artistic products to education, diplomacy, and foreign aid, rather than coercive approaches such as military force and economic sanctions. (These are less applicable to a globalized context in which powerful countries are unlikely to embark on another world war. Today, the emphasis is on cooperation, multilateralism, and stability.)

It is also worth noting that the concept of soft power—if not the term itself—existed long ago. It is often credited to Lao Zi, a Chinese philosopher in the fifth century BC whose teachings formed part of the foundation of China's traditional focus on harmony, good form, and balance. But another Chinese philosopher, Mencius, who was a contemporary of Plato, also defined what today we call soft power:

> When men are subdued by force, it is not that they submit from their hearts but only that their strength is unavailing. When men are won by virtue, then their hearts are gladdened and their submission is sincere.[2]

In the twenty-first century, soft power has become China's method of winning friends and allies as well as support for the country's ambition to be accepted as a world leader. In his keynote speech to the National Congress of the Communist Party of China (CPC) in 2007, President Hu Jintao said that China must "enhance culture as part of the soft power of our country to better guarantee the people's basic cultural rights and interests." He went on to say, "We maintain that the people of all countries should join hands and strive to build a harmonious world of lasting peace and common prosperity."[3]

President Hu's approach to international and domestic affairs is often attributed to Zheng Bijian, his deputy at the Central Party School, the institution that educates each new generation of Chinese leaders. Zheng helped lay the intellectual foundation for Hu's "harmonious world" policy, the cornerstone of the country's soft power initiatives. To understand China it is important to remember that beginning in the ninth century, when neighboring tribes invaded the territory that is known as China today, the country's history has been punctuated by a series of invasions and occupations. If it was not the Mongols (thirteenth to fourteenth centuries), it was the British (who during the Opium Wars of the nineteenth century occupied Shanghai, Nanking, and Hong Kong), or the Japanese (who invaded China for the first time in 1916). In 2003, at a Bo'ao Forum for Asia, Zheng said: "For more than a century ... China was threatened, bullied, invaded and exploited ... Given such a history of suffering, the Chinese want nothing but the important basics: that is, independence, unification, peace, and development."

Thus the appeal of soft power today. Hu's and Zheng's message is echoed by other statesmen. In 2007, Liu Jianchao, former spokesperson for the Ministry of Foreign Affairs (now China's ambassador to the Philippines), said: "We are ready to make joint efforts with people around the globe to build a harmonious world of lasting peace and common prosperity." Former Singapore Prime Minister Lee Kuan Yew has also said: "Soft power is achieved only when other nations admire and want to emulate aspects of that nation's civilization." Singapore certainly is an excellent example of how soft power can help build a nation's image. China is a big fan of soft power. The Japanese also wield it in abundance. South Korean and Indian policymakers are talking about it. A notable initiative that helps project Singapore's soft power is the Tianjin Eco-city project that is being jointly developed with China. The project addresses, among other issues, energy efficiency, waste and water management, and green transportation. This unique experiment aims to create a natural, harmonious, and livable human habitat, a model that will benefit not only other cities in China but also other countries that are facing similar challenges.[4] And in 2009, at the World Economic Forum held in Tianjin, Wang Guoqing, vice minister of the Information Office of the State Council, referred to China's image-building efforts by saying: "Only when we show the world the true China can it agree with our development pattern."

Soft power is also a subject of great interest to various Chinese research institutes and organizations. For example, in 2006, the China Foreign Languages Bureau in Beijing staged a forum on "trans-cultural communications and soft power building." A year later, the International Public Relations Research Center at Fudan University hosted a forum for party officials and leading scholars on "national soft power construction and the development of China's public relations." And the Institute of Strategic Studies of the Central Party School produced a 2007 report titled "Assessment and Report of China's Soft Power."

From my perspective within the business and political communities, I believe Beijing has five priorities:

- Economic development
- Domestic stability
- Maintaining Communist Party control
- International recognition that China is a great nation
- Territorial integrity.

While there is nothing aggressive about any of these objectives, unquestionably, with its new standing in the world, China is ready to assert itself. The shift from the past suggests its leaders recognize that while there is still a place at times for deterrence, the emphasis today is on reassurance. Yes, China's military build-up (which the world has noticed) falls under "deterrence," but far more attention is being paid within China to soft power. China is benefiting from globalization and wants to stand for reform, not warfare.

During the general debate of the UN General Assembly in 2010, Premier Wen Jiabao seized the opportunity to talk about what he described as "the real China." He was responding to an impression that his country's firm response to territorial disputes around that time was a sign of aggression. He wanted to reassure the world that despite China's rising power and influence, it will not seek to dominate other nations; it will continue along the path of peaceful development. As if acknowledging him, U.S. President Barack Obama, whose administration has developed many cooperative relationships with Chinese officials, referred to China as an "outstanding partner."

Soft Rivalry

Today, America's soft power influence is more pervasive than that of any other country. This is because of the universality of the English language and the worldwide popularity of Western cultural exports such as pop music, sports, and Hollywood films. (However, soft power sectors in the United States increasingly look to Asia for both new market opportunities and funding sources.)

Film

China is still developing its popular culture and, at the moment, cannot compete with America. True, in 2009 a total of 315 Chinese films were screened at 119 international film festivals (where 68 of them won 80 awards). And the Beijing-based China Heaven Creation International Performing Arts Company bought a theater in Branson, an entertainment destination in the American Midwest, to stage Chinese-themed shows. But even though many products in the West bear a "Made in China" label, Chinese movies, TV networks, musical groups, fashion designers, companies, and products have not become cultural icons or ubiquitous brand names such as Mickey Mouse, Lady Gaga, Ralph Lauren, Big Mac, CNN, or Microsoft. With a few exceptions, such as NBA star Yao Ming, Gao Xingjian (China's first Nobel Prize-winning novelist), actors Joan Chen, Zhāng Ziyí, and Michelle Yeoh (who is actually a Malaysian Chinese), and movies such as *Hero*; *Crouching Tiger, Hidden Dragon*; and *Farewell My Concubine*, there is still a long road ahead before Chinese cultural products and institutions achieve the West's global reach.

Still, a shift is happening. More and more cash-strapped Hollywood studios look to China and India for financing. The Huayi Group, which Morgan Stanley called "China's Warner Brothers for tomorrow," is developing films with Hollywood majors and, to date, thirty-five Chinese film studios and fifty-eight TV production houses have made the transition from state-owned institutions to private enterprises. Tan Fei, a senior cultural critic and industry insider, said, "An open market helps create more diversification and works of quality, which makes it possible to win a bigger market."[5]

Fashion

The high-profile British-born editor-in-chief of *Vogue* magazine, Anna Wintour (of *The Devil Wears Prada* movie fame), visited Beijing in 2010. As reported by Gary Jones in an article that appeared in the *Post Magazine* of the *South China Morning Post*, she said:

"I wouldn't underestimate anything about this country right now. Whether China will ever have a fashion week on the same scale as Paris or Milan or New York, I couldn't say, but growth here has already been so extraordinary. It's fascinating. There is such an explosion going on. It's fantastic. There is such appetite for fashion." She added, "It seems to me that among young people, there has been an explosion in self-expression here. It's great. And I see a lot of hats. The Chinese seem big on hats."[6]

Steven Meisel, a well-known fashion photographer, shot a group of Asian top models styled by *Vogue*'s creative director, Grace Coddington, and presented as "Asia Major" in the December 2010 issue of *Vogue*. Of the eight models, four came from China—Bonnie Chan, Du Juan, Liu Wen, and Lily Zhi. Liu Wen also appeared in one of Oscar de La Renta's collections.

Designers with ethnic Chinese background are also making their mark in the fashion industry. Names such as Anna Sui, Vivienne Tam, Vera Wang, Jimmy Choo, and Jason Wu (who shot to fame for designing the gown U.S. First Lady Michelle Obama wore to her husband's inauguration ball). The dress has since been inducted into the Smithsonian National Museum of American

History. What current citizenship these talented people hold, I do not know, but Jason Wu was born in Taiwan and Vivienne Tam moved to New York after she graduated from Hong Kong's Polytechnic Fashion School. As reported by Reuters at the Milan Fashion Week, "Chinese designers will drive catwalk trends. . . . as China's creativity becomes fashion's next big thing." The Italian trendsetter designer and retailer Elio Fiorucci said on the sidelines of the Dolce and Gabbana show, "The next big issue for fashion is not China's economic boom but Chinese creativity."[7]

Live Performance

Meanwhile, as part of an ambitious government program called "Chinese Culture Going International," performing arts companies tour abroad with great success. The National Ballet of China, the National Peking Opera Company, and the China Philharmonic Orchestra (ranked by the influential classical music magazine *Gramophone* as one of the "top ten most inspiring orchestras") receive international acclaim when they tour.

China has also promoted cultural exchanges with the United Nations Education, Science and Cultural Organization (UNESCO) and staged events such as Paris China Culture Week (1999), the U.S. Tour of Chinese Culture (2000), the China Festival at Berlin's Asia-Pacific Week (2001), a Chinese cultural tour in Africa (2006), the Year of Russia in China/Year of China in Russia (2007), and the African Culture in Focus/Chinese Culture in Focus (2008–09).

The biggest soft power success of the past decade, of course, was the Beijing Olympics in 2008. China was honored to host the event because it signaled the nation's status as a significant member of the international community. Many of the world-class facilities—such as the "Bird's Nest," where the opening ceremonies were held—resulted from a marriage of Chinese and Western technologies, a further reminder that China was no longer a restrictive and inward-focused nation. And, by demonstrating that it could organize and manage the biggest and most complex sporting event in the world, China consolidated relations with both developed and developing countries.

Values and Rewards

While soft power is often narrowly equated with culture and the arts, it also represents universal values and ideals that can make a country a role model to other nations. With a recorded history of nearly four thousand years, China's traditional culture has been a major influence on East Asia. It is considered one of the four ancient civilizations (the others are Babylon, India, and Egypt), attracting a steady stream of holy men, philosophers, and traders interested in everything from inspiration and wisdom to riches. Today, it is foreign tourists who are increasingly traveling to a country that has grown far more open to visitors than in the recent past. Its arts, handicrafts, and archaeological sites are world famous—including the Great Wall, the Yin Ruins, and the Imperial palaces and tombs of the Ming and Qing Dynasties. The UNESCO World Heritage Committee now lists forty world heritage sites in China (the prestigious global list totals more than nine hundred). China became a member of the World Heritage Convention in 1985, and over the years its Law of Antiquity Protection has been updated and improved.

China's civilization also produced Confucianism, Taoism, Buddhism, and other philosophies whose values tie into the image China wishes to project. Examples include winning respect through virtue (*yi de fu ren*), peace and harmony (*he*), giving priority to human beings (*yi ren wei ben*), doing good to neighbors and treating them as partners (*yulin weishan, yilin weiban*), and achieving harmony despite differences (*he er bu tong*). Given that China has, in the past, been seen by the rest of the world as foreign and threatening, these kinds of values are a strength now that it shares the stage with America as the second world superpower.

China is not entirely a newcomer to world organizations. It was a founding member of the International Monetary Fund in 1945 and assumed a seat at the UN in 1971 as the People's Republic of China. (Previously, the Republic of China had been a member since the founding of the UN in 1945.) The PRC joined the World Bank in 1980 and more recently, in 2001, became part of the WTO. But the shift in China's reputation that has occurred in recent years is perhaps best illustrated by appointments such as those of Margaret Chan, who was named director-general of the World Health Organization in 2006, and Justin Lin, appointed chief economist of the World Bank in 2008. They are the first Chinese to hold top posts in major international organizations.

At one time, China did not see itself as a participant in international affairs. For example, despite having had a seat on the UN Security Council since 1971, for years it did not participate in UN peacekeeping operations. This was largely because of the dynamics between the Cold War superpowers (the United States and the Soviet Union) and because of its longstanding position on nonintervention. But a shift in policy began as the Cold War thawed. Over the past two decades China has taken part in eighteen UN peacekeeping operations and contributed fifteen thousand civilian police officers, military observers, engineers, medical specialists, and other personnel. As of this writing, two thousand Chinese peacekeepers are involved in ten UN operations worldwide.

Shortly before the Millennium Development Goals (MDG) Summit in September 2010, UN Secretary-General Ban Ki-moon told journalists that China is playing an important role in the preservation of peace and security around the world. As reported by various media, Ban added, "The whole world is looking to the UN and also to China for its contribution." And the country has responded. China sent its own search-and-rescue teams to Haiti and Chile after earthquakes hit those countries and has assisted in postwar reconstruction efforts in Afghanistan. It has been active in encouraging nuclear nonproliferation agreements for Korea and Iraq. As far as China's own military activities are concerned, the newest twist is a 10,000-ton hospital ship, modeled after two American vessels—the USNS *Comfort* and USNS *Mercy*. It will provide medical care and emergency services for humanitarian purposes and, in addition, is meant to soften China's image abroad as a potentially hostile nation.

The MDGs are a set of international development goals directed at developing nations that include eliminating extreme poverty and child mortality, expanding universal education, and combating diseases such as HIV/AIDS, malaria, and tuberculosis by 2015. These issues were agreed to by 189 world leaders in 2000. Ban praised China for supporting many developing nations with economic assistance. According to the UN Development Program's Regional Bureau for Asia and Pacific, China has achieved the MDG targets of halving the impoverished population and providing universal primary education, as well as having made real progress in areas such as health and gender equality. The conclusion: China will likely achieve all its MDG targets by 2015.

Klaus Schwab, founder and chairman of the World Economic Forum, praised China in an exclusive interview with *China Daily*. He said, "China's voice should be better heard in the international community, but it is also very important for China to use its soft power not only at official conferences but also at unofficial meetings, such as this forum, to help shape global opinion and global decisions. I also think it is very important that China plays an intensive and strong part in informal causes, exercising soft power, influencing decision makers and public opinion by presenting legitimate views as a strong global power."[8]

China is involved in many partnerships in developing nations, often where Beijing has an interest in natural resources. This is not new. The 806-kilometers (501-miles) Karakoram Highway in Pakistan was completed with China's assistance back in the early seventies, as was the TAZARA railway connecting Tanzania and Zambia (built with one million tons of equipment and materials from China, which also dispatched fifty thousand engineering and technical workers to help with the project). But more recently, with an intensified interest in soft power, China has helped Myanmar with an upgrade of its national telecommunication network, built low-income homes—nicknamed "China Village"—in Angola, and funded the Lesotho National Library in the Kingdom of Lesotho, a small country surrounded by South Africa. The 150-bed Sino-Congolese Friendship Hospital, completed with Chinese financing and technical assistance, was among the first modern medical centers in the Democratic Republic of the Congo.

In the closing two years of the twentieth century, China signed many international deals and announced many proposals that involved major development projects in Africa. State-owned firms announced the building of a $4 billion port in Kenya. There was news about the purchase of a third of the petroleum assets previously owned by the United Kingdom's Tullow Oil in Uganda for

$1.25 billion. Chinese developers signed an agreement to invest up to $23 billion to build oil refineries in Nigeria. And an agreement was reached with two local partners to build a $217 million cement plant in South Africa. In 2010, by the time these projects were well under way or even completed, a number of African nations signed financing agreements with China's Export-Import Bank, among them Ghana, Zambia, Ethiopia, Mozambique, and Angola, for a variety of new projects.

To focus on just one example, China's involvement in the Democratic Republic of the Congo illustrates the ambitious and complex scope of its international investment strategy. A mineral-rich nation, Congo is nonetheless sub-Saharan Africa's poorest country because of a deadly combination of war and unconstrained corruption. Today, a consortium of Chinese companies is involved in infrastructure projects worth $6 billion—roughly half of the central African state's GDP. These projects include building copper and cobalt mines, railways, roads, schools, hospitals, and health clinics. Congolese public officials select Chinese construction firms—backed by Beijing—to do the work quickly and without risk of corruption. It is not an overstatement to say that China alone represents the Congo's economic future. How does China benefit? It will get badly needed resources: 11 million tons of copper and 620,000 tons of cobalt, all of which will be extracted over the next quarter century.

Trade

According to the Chinese Ministry of Commerce, the country's trade with Africa exceeded $100 billion in 2010. More than 1,600 Chinese businesses were investing in Africa, mainly in the mining, agricultural, construction, and manufacturing sectors. In February 2011, Standard Bank Group, Ltd., a South Africa-based international financial services institution, predicted that China's investment in Africa would hit $50 billion by 2015, a 70 percent increase from 2009. Meanwhile, bilateral trade between China and Africa will reach $300 billion by 2015, double the 2010 level.

"No country has made as big an impact on the political, economic and social fabric of Africa as China has since the turn of the millennium," wrote economist Dambisa Moyo in her 2009 book, *Dead Aid: Why Aid Is Not Working and How There Is a Better Way for Africa*. Moyo believes that the history of Western foreign aid, with its emphasis on grants and loans rather than investment and its demands for human rights reforms and improved governance, was both overly restrictive and moralistic. In fact, China presents itself as a better partner for developing countries in Africa since it, too, is in many ways still a developing nation. (For example, China offers more advantageous terms on its loans, compared to Western companies.) To Moyo, China's hands-off approach—mutually beneficial, market-driven business arrangements and a noninvolvement policy toward domestic affairs—stands a better chance of improving overall conditions in Africa.

Still, China's economic strategy in Africa may cause some damage to its international reputation. Even Chinese officials realize that their unconditional approach raises the possibility of tacitly supporting corrupt dictatorships, which could lead to both political and financial risks. (Chinese companies that invested in Libya, for example, were all too aware of their vulnerability during the 2011 political unrest.)

In what will probably be a sign of things to come, in 2010 the World Bank announced that its private sector division, the International Finance Corporation (IFC), had signed its first agreement to finance Chinese investment in Africa. The project—an office development in Dar es Salaam, Tanzania—is modest but symbolic. By cooperating with the IFC, China benefits from the World Bank's international reputation, and other investors are more likely to get on board with China. At the same time, the IFC connection sends a message that China is concerned about its own corporate governance, environmental issues, and human rights standards. And it is a sign that China's growing stature as a world power will include close involvement with existing multilateral institutions.

Where is China's investment going in the future? A good source of information is the China Global Investment Tracker, a comprehensive database of Chinese investments published by the Heritage Foundation, a U.S. conservative think tank. In a report published in February 2011, the volume of investment was reported to have exceeded $200 billion over five years. The report also showed that the trend is toward investment in the Western Hemisphere outside of the United States. Once a minor part of China's strategy, today the leading regions of Chinese spending are Brazil (by far the largest at $14.9 billion), Canada ($10.2 billion), and Venezuela ($8.9 billion).[9]

Education and Travel

Another form of soft power is education. I still remember, years ago, being a college student in the United States and hearing a common joke of the era that began "Confucius say . . ."—spoken with an exaggerated Chinese accent. Today, the interest in the Chinese language and culture is no laughing matter. China has opened more than 300 Confucius institutes and 272 Confucius classrooms in 88 countries with a total of about 260,000 students having gone through these programs. The stated goal is "promoting Chinese language and culture and supporting local Chinese teaching."

In this way these initiatives are similar to organizations such as Alliance Française, the Cervantes Institute, the British Council, and the Goethe Institute, all of which provide language lessons, teaching opportunities, and cultural information. But China's ambitious educational outreach is also a potent form of soft power, increasing China's reputation and popularity and creating a population of educated, Chinese-speaking foreign professionals who will have a much better understanding of China.

When I studied in America in the 1950s, I was among a relatively small number of ambitious young people from China getting an education abroad. Today, hundreds of thousands of undergraduate and graduate students from China are studying in the West. However, more and more often you can see American and European business schools, for example, advertising in Hong Kong, Beijing, and Shanghai. Some of them have joint ventures or other cooperative tie-ins with universities in Asia. The Kellogg School at Northwestern, for instance, has established a very successful EMBA program with the Hong Kong University of Science and Technology.

Many leading institutions in Hong Kong and mainland China have created special scholarship programs designed to reverse the trend by attracting highly ranked international students to study in China. Education is a focus of international projects as well. In 2003, China helped Egypt complete the first phase of its long-distance education project, which covered twenty-seven provinces. And in 2007, China helped complete the second phase, which more than quadrupled the number of teaching centers in Egypt to 143. In many poor nations, China promotes learning Chinese in primary schools and offers scholarships to attend universities in China to those who excel. Exchanges with African countries, which began in the 1950s but have expanded substantially over the past decade, involve about six thousand African students enrolling in Chinese universities, where they learn Chinese and study technical subjects such as engineering.

By the end of 2009, China had built more than a hundred schools in developing countries and provided scholarships to more than seventy thousand overseas students. Today, anywhere from 120,000 to 140,000 foreign students are studying in China. The country also sent more than two thousand teachers abroad and trained ten thousand instructors and headmasters.

In February 2010, one week after Premier Wen Jiabao pledged to make China's universities "world class," the president of Yale University, Richard Levin, predicted in the *Guardian* that China's elite universities could be among the world's top ten within a quarter of a century, rivaling Oxford and Cambridge in the United Kingdom and the Ivy League institutions in the United States.[10] At the moment, six Chinese universities rank among the top hundred international universities (three in Hong Kong that are among the top fifty, as well as two in mainland China and one in Taiwan). In fact, Beijing is spending 1.5 percent of its GDP on higher education. But to be counted among the elite of the world, China's universities will have to achieve a multi-disciplinary breadth and cultivate critical thinking that is not quite present at this time.

The Chinese Ministry of Education estimates that about twenty thousand American students are currently studying in China. (Many stay for a short time to learn the language, as compared to Chinese students studying in America, who tend to remain to complete an undergraduate degree and often do postgrad work as well.) During

President Obama's visit to China in November 2009, he pledged to increase that number to a hundred thousand (although he did not specify a time frame). Speaking to a group of students in Shanghai, he said, "The research we share, the business we do, the knowledge we gain and even the sports we play, these bridges must be built by young men and women just like you and your counterparts in the U.S."

My youngest daughter is among the more than one hundred thousand Chinese students studying in America. A junior at Claremont McKenna College in California—one of the top U.S. liberal arts colleges—she once asked me, "Why are you sending me all the way over to America when all three of Hong Kong's leading universities are ranked among the top fifty in the world?" I realized this was not an easy question to answer. Finally I replied, "Treat your four years in America as an experience in your journey through life. If, upon graduating, you decide you prefer China to the American way of life and culture, we will welcome you home with open arms."

At this stage, my youngest daughter expresses an interest in returning to Hong Kong. Many others of her age, however, prefer to stay in the United States—something that is not always simple to arrange. According to a cover story in *China Daily*, twenty-two-year-old Yvonne Liu wanted to remain in the United States after her studies, so her mother, who has a trading business, decided to establish a branch office in southern California by investing a minimum of $500,000. Through the EB-5 investor visa program, her daughter can get a green card. People such as Yvonne Liu are China's "soft power ambassadors."[11]

Sometimes, what is most impressive is the enthusiasm and energy of young people. A friend of my youngest daughter launched, with some friends, an organization called Global China Connection. It is dedicated to building bridges and forging friendships between the Western world and China through cultural and language exchange programs. GCC works with top Chinese universities to help foreign students learn Chinese, and it arranges accommodations, insurance, social activities, and interaction with native speakers. When I heard about this, I thought, what a worthwhile initiative, with no political involvement at all, to help the West meet the East.

A final note here about tourism. The China National Tourism Administration estimates that between now and 2015, a hundred million overseas trips will be taken by Chinese tourists, who will spend approximately $100 billion. These, too, will be China's "soft power ambassadors." Unfortunately, many are not well versed in Western etiquette. New to traveling abroad, they may spit on the streets, cut ahead of others in queues, smoke intensely, or speak in inappropriately loud voices. This will give an impression of ill manners and pushiness, although Western countries will put up with it for the sake of tourism dollars. It will probably take a generation for Chinese tourists to become sophisticated travelers. In the meantime, we will ask for your patience.

Spreading the Word

Practicing soft power is one thing, but it is equally important to communicate it to the world. In a February 2010 article titled "The New Public Diplomacy," Joseph Nye wrote: "The world of traditional power politics was typically about whose military or economy would win. In today's information age, politics is also about whose 'story' wins."[12] And in late 2008, Li Changchun, a member of the Communist Party's top ruling body, said, "Enhancing our communication capacity domestically and internationally is of direct consequence to our nation's international influence and international position."

To that end, the Chinese government created a new Office of Public Diplomacy within the Foreign Ministry. At the same time, the State Council Information Office is in charge of facilitating and coordinating efforts to get China's message to the world by encouraging scholars, organizations, and journalists to be more active and effective in the world of think tanks and the international media.

When it comes to communications, American dominance of mass media has been a great advantage, allowing the United States to control the agenda for decades. The four major Western news agencies—Associated Press, United Press International, Reuters, and Agence France-Presse—are responsible for four-fifths of the news generated in the world each day. The United States alone produces three-quarters of all TV programs in the world.

In a bid to raise China's voice on the world stage and compete with Western media, Beijing has provided a reported $8.7 billion, mainly to the four leading state-run media outlets: Xinhua News Agency, the *China Daily* newspaper, China Central Television (CCTV), and China Radio International (CRI) to expand abroad. For example, CCTV, which has six international channels in five languages, including English, is said to have a total audience of about 125 million. It is positioning itself to compete with CNN and the BBC. Xinhua is adding to its 117 foreign bureaus and network of 400 foreign-based journalists.

Today, Xinhua has eighty thousand paying institutional subscribers and is the primary source of international news in Africa. And in July 2010, Xinhua launched CNC World, a second international English-language TV channel available via satellite and the Internet. (Part of China's shift to world power status includes encouraging competition.) There is even a plan to build a newsroom atop a skyscraper in New York's Times Square to provide exposure in America.

Meanwhile, CRI is purchasing airtime in radio markets in the United States and Europe, besides broadcasting directly into the Middle East, Africa, and Latin America. So, at a time when the Voice of America has reduced its Chinese broadcasts from nineteen to fourteen hours daily, CRI is increasing its English broadcasts to twenty-four hours a day. (Speaking of English, language can be a barrier to China's progress. In my view, Chinese leaders should use English more often, rather than using translators when they communicate with countries around the world. Like it or not, English is still the common denominator of global communication and international diplomacy.)

Part of this overall media strategy has been a concerted program that began in 2009 when twenty handpicked postgraduate students (with master's degrees in journalism) from five leading universities were assigned to Xinhua, CCTV, and the English-language *China Daily*. They were the first in a wave of students to receive multi-disciplinary training specifically aimed at extending China's international reach. The idea is to make China's media less propagandistic, emphasizing serious journalism and more diversified coverage.

I am not sure how all this culture sharing will unfold, but I suspect China will make progress across the soft power areas, just as America will continue to lead for years to come. For example, even though China is courting Latin American countries—often successfully—the geopolitical reality is very hard to overcome. Kevin Casas-Zamora, a Latin America expert with the Brookings Institute, said, "The U.S. and Latin America are doomed to live closely together and China can never compete with that; there are simply cultural and geographical barriers."[13] What he means is that America's soft power appeal, resonating through popular culture, language, images, and ideals, will overwhelm China's efforts. And when it comes to hard power, for the foreseeable future most nations facing times of trouble still call Washington first, not Beijing.

Is China's soft power strategy working? A 2007 BBC poll found that twice as many nations believed China has a mostly positive influence on the world as compared to the United States. That is quite a shift from the authoritarian days of Mao, when the Western world knew little about China, and what it did know it didn't like. But this may give proof to Joseph Nye's observation, "Seduction is almost always more effective than coercion." China's various initiatives to improve its international image and forge partnerships abroad have been called "public diplomacy" (*gonggong waijiao*), "good neighbor diplomacy" (*mulin waijiao*), or "smile diplomacy" (*weixiao waijiao*). But regardless of the name, it's all soft power. President Hu's state visit to America in January 2011, coupled with a visit to Chicago, was certainly soft power at work. The television advertisement in Times Square, New York, was just an added touch. In the end, it is all about perception.

8

CLIMBING THE
TECHNOLOGY LADDER

FROM "ASSEMBLED IN CHINA" TO
"INNOVATED IN CHINA"

About half a century ago, after I graduated from the Wharton School of Business with an MBA, I worked for a year as a management trainee at IBM. The company, already a pioneer in computer technology, had introduced its 1400 series, the second generation of midrange business computers. Compared to today, of course, they were crude machines with magnetic tape for input and line printers for output. But they were state-of-the-art at a time when America was the undisputed world leader in computers. Around this same time, IBM pioneered magnetic disk storage, a critical element of the emerging technological revolution that would reshape the world.

By contrast, China's computer industry did not get started until the late 1950s, when a vacuum-tube machine called the "901" was made at the Institute of Military Engineering at the University of Harbin (now known as Harbin Engineering University) in Heilongjiang Province. China continued to lag behind developed nations until the past decade—but the gap has started to close. Now another breathtaking shift in power has happened. A scientific research center in China—a nation until recently considered a high-tech backwater—has built the fastest supercomputer ever made.

In November 2010, the National University of Defense Technology announced that its Tianhe-1A, which is housed in the National Center for Supercomputing in Tianjin, near Beijing, operates at speeds 43 percent faster than preceding systems and is capable of making 2,507 trillion calculations per second. Perhaps equally important is the fact that the Tianhe-1A replaces the previous fastest supercomputer—the U.S.-made Jaguar, installed at the Oak Ridge National Laboratory in Tennessee. (The United States had lost its status as the supercomputing leader only once before, in 2002, when Japan unveiled a faster machine. Two years later, after a massive investment program, the United States regained the crown and kept it until the Tianhe-1A.)[1]

This technological breakthrough is a victory for China in many ways. Building the world's fastest supercomputer is a source of national pride. The machines are valued for their ability to solve problems in such key areas as defense, energy, finance, medicine, and science. Oil and gas companies use them to find new reserves, and stock markets rely on them for instantaneous trading. They are also critically important for large-scale weather forecasting, which tracks hurricanes and measures and predicts global climate change. Like most supercomputers, the Tianhe-1A relies on many thousands of chips made by the U.S. companies Intel and Nvidia, but the real breakthrough came with networking technology developed by Chinese researchers.

The supercomputer may, however, have other benefits for China. The Tianhe-1A is one of twenty-four Chinese systems on the list of the world's five hundred most powerful supercomputers. As a result, China has risen to third place, behind the United States and the European Union, in overall high-performance computing power. Nations with state-of-the-art supercomputers attract top scientific and engineering talent from around the world. So the prospects going forward look very bright.

On a lighter side, the *South China Morning Post* reported early in 2011 that an IBM high-performance computer (named Watson in honor of IBM's founder) beat two champions of the U.S. popular quiz show, *Jeopardy!* in a landmark man-versus-machine challenge. John Kelly, an IBM senior vice president and director of research operations, said the company's scientists in China were "very significant contributors," who developed software that helped the computer process natural human language and deliver answers to complex questions quickly.[2]

But there is another side to technology. With the emergence of Microsoft in 1975 and its extraordinary rise to its present power and influence, technological innovation began permeating every facet of daily life, from person-to-person communication to the way in which business is now conducted. The ongoing integration of communications platforms—from e-mail to instant messaging to mobile phones with their ever-expanding voice-enabled applications to cloud computing—is mindboggling. This continuous stream of innovative and hard-to-resist gadgets will continue to have an impact on the social fabric of societies around the world.

China, not surprisingly, is now becoming one of the leaders of this high-tech explosion. In 2008, Huawei, the country's leading communications device maker, filed the world's largest number of applications for international patents and trademarks. In 2010, it startled European and U.S. companies when it completed negotiations on a deal to build a Long Term Evolution (LTE) mobile network in Sweden, a country dominated by telecom giant Ericsson. Along with China's rise as an economic superpower, another powerful shift has occurred. The country can now credibly claim its place in the technological big leagues.

Now that China has come through the global recession with minimal damage, it is in the process of reclaiming its former reputation. In the summer of 2010, China passed Japan to become the second-largest economy in the world and, if analysts are correct, it will displace the United States in the not-too-distant future. At that time, it will return to its former glory as the leading global powerhouse. After all, it held this position for approximately 1,500 years until the Industrial Revolution of the mid-nineteenth century, when Britain became the world leader (and modern British warships steamed up the Yangtze River).

Today, with a decline in China's exports to those Western countries still struggling to get out of the economic downturn, Beijing has shifted its focus to domestic consumption. Its leaders' most important task is to sustain its growth and development and provide employment for its huge population. At the same time, with wages rising and inflationary pressures always present, the country has moved toward a new stage of development, one that will have a profound impact on China and the West.

For several years now, China has been quietly shifting from being primarily an economy based on low-cost factories to becoming a sophisticated high-technology economy as well. Low-cost manufacturing is still important, because some of the factories have migrated to the western part of the country, where low-cost labor still exists. But as wages rise, another phenomenon will occur: some firms producing low-cost exports may become so uncompetitive that they will move their factories offshore, to countries such as Indonesia, Thailand, Vietnam, or India. In the face of this, the government will still need to maintain growth around 9 percent and provide employment for the better-educated, technologically savvy young generation on the rise.

For example, Shenzhen, located in Guangdong Province immediately north of Hong Kong, was China's first special economic zone, making it a key hub for low-cost manufacturing. But by encouraging firms to consolidate market share and gain economies of scale (which can also mean combining resources for research and development), Beijing wants to encourage the area to climb up the value chain. New labor laws, minimum wage rulings, and rising prices for raw materials contribute to drive those making low-value products—especially those that have a severe impact on the environment—to relocate further west. Today, Shenzhen, with its population of ten million, is being developed into a high-tech zone, and leading Hong Kong universities are setting up campuses across the border to support this initiative.

Research and Development

As is true throughout the industrialized world, research and development is a top priority. China's investment in R&D was more than 580 billion yuan ($87.2 billion) in 2010. According to the Paris-based Organization for Economic Cooperation and Development, it ranks third in gross expenditures on R&D, slightly behind the United States and Japan. By 2020, China's R&D expenditures are projected to reach 2.5 percent of GDP (very close to the 2.7 percent level of the United States). Furthermore, over the past several years university enrollments in science and engineering at both the undergraduate and graduate level have increased by nearly 30 percent annually. A study in November 2010 by the information firm Thomson Reuters suggests China is now second only to the United States at producing scholarly scientific papers.

China's large companies are obviously engaged in R&D, but the difference is that the majority of these enterprises are state-owned. The Chinese government offers incentives such as accelerated depreciation on investments in R&D facilities and tax breaks on returns from venture capital projects that are tech-based start-ups. State-owned banks offer cheaper loans to help develop domestic technologies, which can then replace imported ones, and procurement policies are designed to favor indigenously developed technologies.

The central government also requires foreign-owned multinational companies to form joint ventures with state-owned Chinese companies and share their technologies as a condition of entry into the market. This requirement is not always welcome in Western boardrooms, but it is certainly understandable. Despite China's large trade surpluses with the West, foreign companies have traditionally reaped the profits and, to date, they have also dominated most of China's high-tech industries. Contrary thinking would suggest that state-owned enterprises might lack the ambition to be truly innovative. However, this increased government incentive and support is only continued for enterprises with a proven track record of innovation.

One particularly innovative program launched by the Chinese government in 2008 was called "Thousand Talents." It targets top Chinese and foreign scientists, engineers, and academics working at the world's major institutions or as entrepreneurs and encourages them to come to China to lead research projects at universities, join corporate labs, or start their own businesses. Each recruit receives up to 10 million yuan ($1.5 million) from the central government as well as funding from their employers. They are called "sea turtles" or *hai gui* in Chinese because of their tendency to return to their place of birth. According to the Boston-based Monitor Consultancy, some eighty thousand Western-trained

Chinese scientists have returned home to work in academia or industry since the mid-1980s.

Sector by Sector

China's R&D push is especially visible in certain sectors of industry. Some of these sectors that have been making headlines include air transportation, high-speed rail, electric cars, and the country's space program, as well as power generation and information technology.

Aviation

All the Chinese airlines have been buying large jets from Boeing and Airbus, while the smaller (fifty- to hundred-seat) market has been dominated by Canada's Bombardier and Brazil's Embraer. China attempted to move into this industry through a licensing arrangement with McDonnell Douglas to build the MD-80 (and later MD-90) series of medium-range passenger jets. The initiative began in 1985 and, by 1994, more than thirty planes had been delivered. The partnership was eventually terminated when Boeing acquired McDonnell Douglas in 1997 and sophisticated machine tools were sold to a Chinese company.

Since that time, China has been through several restructurings in its aviation industry, resulting in the formation in 2008 of Commercial Aircraft Corporation of China (COMAC). Today, COMAC is designing and building commercial aircraft to reduce the country's dependence on foreign firms. The first delivery of the ARJ 21 Xiangfeng series of twin-engine regional jets was announced in November 2010 at the China International Aviation and Aerospace Exhibition in Zhuhai (across the border from Hong Kong). COMAC also unveiled the prototype for its C919, which is intended to compete in the Boeing 737 and Airbus 320 categories of larger passenger jets. Four Chinese airlines—Air China, China Southern, China Eastern, and Hainan Airlines—together with GE Capital Aviation Services (whose parent firm, General Electric, is providing engines for the aircraft in partnership with France's Safran Group) and China Development Bank

Leasing jointly made a commitment to buy one hundred C919s when they come onstream.

Also on display in Zhuhai was the jet-powered WJ600 from China Aerospace Science & Industry. This drone seems to be of greatest concern to the United States because the technology involved in its creation is considered to be the future of military aviation.

According to Giovanni Bisignani, director general and CEO of the International Air Transport Association, which represents some 230 airlines around the world, the industry could soon be replacing the existing international civil aviation agreement—the so-called Chicago Convention—with perhaps a Beijing Convention. The Chicago Convention has governed the international air transport industry since 1947. It not only set up the International Civil Aviation Organization, a UN agency that coordinates and regulates international air travel, but also established airspace rules, aircraft registration, and safety standards. Bisignani, who is retiring and will be replaced by Tony Tyler, Cathay Pacific's CEO, believes that airlines should be able to fly where the traffic is and that airlines should be able to run like a normal business. Currently there are still considerable restrictions on aircraft routes and airline ownership. For example, the United States imposes a 25 percent ownership limit on U.S. carriers, the EU cap is 49 percent.

China is today the fastest-growing market for international and domestic passengers. Air China is the world's largest carrier with a market capitalization of $20 billion. China is also moving toward using biofuels in aircraft with a tie-up between Air China and PetroChina.

High-Speed Rail

In the early 1990s, when Beijing realized that commercial train service was losing market share to the country's network of highways as well as air travel, it began a modernization campaign to create high-speed rail lines. Beginning in 1997, there have been six rounds of speed-up campaigns designed to upgrade existing track so trains could reach speeds of up to 160 kilometers an hour

(100 miles per hour). How slow that seems today! China has the world's longest high-speed rail network, with more than 7,000 kilometers 4,350 miles of service routes, including nearly 2,000 kilometers 1,250 miles of rail lines with top speeds of 350 kph (220 mph). And during a trial run in September 2010, a new high-speed train linking Shanghai and Hangzhou set a world record of 416.6 kph (269 mph).

By 2013, the travel time between Beijing and most of the country's capital cities will be significantly reduced. According to the planning department at the Ministry of Railways, for example, it will take just half an hour to reach Tianjin and Shijiazhuang from Beijing, two hours to reach Shenyang, Jinan, Zhenzhou, Taiyuan, and Hohhot, and only eight hours to reach distant cities such as Kunming, Haikou, Nanning, Urumqi, Lhasa, Hong Kong, and Macao. These are all trips that once took at least twice that length of time.

Today, China is negotiating with seventeen other countries in Asia and Eastern Europe to connect to the existing railway infrastructure in the EU. Additional lines would be built into Southeast Asia as well as Russia. The financing will be provided by China in exchange for natural resources from the various partner nations. For China, this will mean faster and more efficient transportation of goods into its own manufacturing centers. At the same time, partner nations will reap the benefits of a high-speed, low-carbon transportation system. Imagine, one day passengers will be able to travel from King's Cross Station in London to Beijing in just two days. There is recent news that China is considering merging its two dominant state-owned railway equipment producers to lead a high-speed rail export drive. If this materializes, the revenues of the combined group would exceed global competitors such as Bombardier, Alstom, and Siemens. What a difference compared to the Silk Road days.

Electric Cars

A number of factors have converged and inspired China's government to transform the country into the world's leader in electric car technology. Increasingly prosperous, the Chinese bought approximately 16 million new vehicles in 2010, a 41 percent increase over the preceding year and 40 percent more than the number of cars sold in the United States over the same period. There are currently 65 million cars and trucks in China, and experts predict there will be ten times that by 2050. However, fuel is very expensive. With about 19 percent of the world's population, China has less than 1 percent of its oil reserves. (It imports about two-thirds of the oil it uses.) And there are environmental concerns. Electric cars consume less fossil fuel than traditional vehicles, and their use generates less greenhouse gas.

One area where Chinese automakers have an advantage is in lithium-ion batteries, the key strategic technology for electric vehicles. Back in the 1980s, the United States decided to leave most consumer electronics manufacturing to Asia, where the work was being done much more cost-effectively. As a result, America lost a leadership role in areas such as the batteries that today power everything from cell phones and laptops to electric cars. In China there are now thirty times as many people working in the lithium battery industry as there are in the United States.

As a result, Beijing plans to spend $15 billion on R&D over the next decade to subsidize this industry, including the building of plants and infrastructure. And in April 2010, China's oldest car manufacturer, the state-owned First Automotive Industry announced that it plans to invest nearly $3 billion in R&D over the next five years to expand its capacity. The company will not have to look far to find a market. In May 2010, Shenzhen became the first Chinese city to put all-electric taxis into operation. The city officially launched thirty battery-powered cabs based on local carmaker BYD's e6 model. Subsequently, the number was increased to one hundred. By 2012, the city aims to have 2,400 of these electric cabs on the road.[3]

Power Grid

China is planning to spend hundreds of billions of yuan in the next few years to upgrade its extensive power distribution network so it can improve energy efficiency and lower greenhouse gas emissions. The upgrade will increase the power grid's efficiency by 20 percent and help save 70 billion kWh in two decades. This would be equal to saving 32 million tons of coal, or removing 69 million tons of carbon dioxide and 3.9 million tons of sulfur dioxide from the air.

China is the world's largest market for power transmission and transformation equipment. Global players such as ABB, Siemens, and Areva T&D have set up plants in the country. Domestic companies, however, are catching up with intensive R&D and support by the central government. As a result, local transformer manufacturers have acquired the technology and expertise to produce globally competitive equipment.

Space Program

China is spending billions of dollars on the most ambitious and diverse manned and unmanned space research and development in the world. These include manned flights, a second lunar orbiter mission, and the development of a nuclear-powered common lunar lander bus designed to support Chinese lunar operations and unmanned return flights by 2013.

In September 2010, China announced that the country would be carrying out explorations into deep space by bringing moon rock samples back to Earth by 2017 and sending a man to the moon by 2025. There are also plans for an observatory to be built on the surface of the moon, as well as continued development of the Hard X-ray Modulation Telescope, with plans to launch it into space by 2012. (It is designed to identify black holes and neutron stars.) And in a marked change from the secretive past, officials have expressed a willingness to share their knowledge and work with the United States.

Innovation Across the Board

Innovation does not necessarily happen only in the more sophisticated technology sectors. In fact, a January 2011 *Financial Times* article talked about how emerging markets are providing Western multinationals with not only faster growth prospects but also new products as well as manufacturing processes. The article used the latest successful entry in the highly competitive soft drinks market—a brand called Pulpy—as an example. Introduced in China by the Minute Maid unit of Coca-Cola, Pulpy has now been rolled out across Asia and South America, with Eastern Europe next on its expansion plan. As the article indicated, "These innovations do not yet involve transformational technological shifts—such inventions remain the preserve of the developed world with its long established universities and commercial laboratories. But the emerging world is spawning product improvements with commercial implications that are game changing."[4]

Some complain that Chinese companies steal technology in a government-backed modernization drive. But many of these technologies were shared in joint ventures. In fact, Chinese companies are now beginning to enter world markets, often working with their Western partners. China's CSR, for example, is working with GE and Siemens in bidding for high-speed rail contracts around the world, which will help create badly needed jobs in the West.

There are also home-grown breakthroughs. In a February 2011 issue of the *South China Morning Post*, the headline was "Traditional Medicine and Findings from West Led to Breakthrough," followed by "2-Yuan Cure for Acute Leukaemia Earns Doctor Top Science Honor."[5] Hematologist Wang Zhenyi has been treating patients with all-trans retinoic acid plus arsenic—a poison but a common ingredient in traditional Chinese medicine. More than 95 percent of his patients have recovered within five years without any need for chemotherapy. His discovery has won him a State Scientific and Technological Award, presented by President Hu Jintao.

The eighty-six-year-old doctor is the former director of Ruijin Hospital's Shanghai Institute of Haematology under Shanghai Jiao Tong University. In the early 1980s, he read a report on research by some American doctors who had found that some APL cells affected by ATRA could mutate to normal ones. He was taken by surprise at the success of his ensuing experiments with the drug when he combined it with arsenic.

Wang refused to apply for the intellectual property rights to his remedy, and he made sure news spread overseas. According to the Ruijin Hospital's publicity office, among fifty-four patients who underwent Wang's method in France in 1993, the complete remission rate was 91 percent.

Two years later, when 79 patients in the United States were treated, that rate was 86 percent. Also in 1995, ATRA was prescribed for 109 patients in Japan, of whom 89 percent achieved complete remission.

Online Development

China's transformation in the age of that other great technological revolution, the Internet, is perhaps the most complex and challenging shift to occur in the country's modern history. It is a story with an impact on both business and culture.

In a now familiar trend, during the past dozen years major American multinationals—including Yahoo, eBay, Microsoft's MSN, AOL, Amazon.com, MySpace, YouTube, Facebook, and Twitter—have all attempted to penetrate the Chinese market. They met with little success, partly due to regulatory hurdles, but mostly because they tended to be too focused on short-term profits and failed to empower their local management. In addition, most wanted to stick to doing business as they were accustomed to operating in the West. Unwilling to tailor their approach to the local market, they wound up giving an advantage to local competitors.

Today this sector is dominated by local players such as Internet commerce leader Alibaba Group, instant messaging giant Tencent, and Baidu, China's leading search engine. These three companies combined have a market capitalization of over $100 billion. Although at first the Chinese were disinclined to pay with anything except cash, online payment mechanisms are now fully established with Alipay, credit cards, debit cards, and COD, all supplied by robust shipping services nationwide.

The market they reach is similarly impressive. There are more than 420 million Internet users in China—nearly one-quarter of the world's total—and nearly 300 million Chinese accessing the Internet via cell phones. People using the Internet describe it as *geili*, which would literally translate as "giving power," but this is a slang term among young online users that actually means "cool" or "awesome." (In the viral way that things spread on the Internet, it has even been turned into an English word, *ungelivable*.) In a move that surprised many, the *People's Daily* even featured the word in a headline on its front page late in 2010. This was highly unusual because online jargon is usually considered too informal for standard written language, especially in the official organ of the Central Committee of the Communist Party of China.[6]

According to a May 2010 report by the Boston Consulting Group (BCG), Chinese users spend approximately a billion hours online each day. That's more than double the daily total in the United States, and this number is expected to grow to more than two billion hours a day by 2015. More than 80 percent of Chinese consumers use instant messaging, read news online, and download or stream music and videos via the Internet. The study also showed that although young professionals make up only 6 percent of all Chinese Internet users, they have an astonishing 99 percent rate of penetration and are the heaviest users (averaging four hours a day online).[7]

One of the most significant changes in online behavior in the past few years has been the growth of e-commerce, which resulted in the success story behind Taobao.com, the consumer-to-consumer (C2C) site owned by Alibaba Group. In 2009, C2C transactions in China represented $37 billion, and BCG predicts that number will exceed $100 billion within three years. E-commerce use is expected to reach 19 percent of the Chinese population by 2012. Multinationals, which must operate in China through partnerships with locally owned firms, will have to adapt to the Chinese business environment if they hope to profit from this shift toward digital media, which is gaining in momentum at a very high speed.

One multinational conspicuous by its absence is Google. A defining moment in China's Internet history was the public row with Google that exploded in late 2009.

Here it's necessary to backtrack for a moment to understand the roots of that incident. Founded in 1998, Google runs the world's most popular search engine, which has not only made the company hugely profitable but has given it tremendous influence online. But Google is not just a search engine. The company's mission includes organizing the world's information and making it universally accessible. Nonetheless, when Google first established its Chinese operation in 2005 it set it up in such a way that the search results met the government's censorship laws.

(Something it was criticized for in the West.) Still, things went wrong, as has been made evident in a white paper published by Google in November 2010. Without singling out China, the paper stated, "In addition to infringing on human rights, governments that block the free flow of information on the Internet are also blocking trade and economic growth."

The controversy began in March 2009 when Chinese officials blocked access to Google's popular YouTube site. After this decision, Google reported that more of its services had been blocked from time to time. In January 2010, the company announced it had been hacked—allegedly along with other U.S. technology firms in China. At that point, Google refused to continue censoring searches in China. Instead, it redirected search queries to its operation in Hong Kong, bypassing Chinese regulatory laws because that city's independent judicial power meant it was not subject to the same Internet restrictions. The standoff ended in March 2010 when Google's license was renewed so long as the company agreed to stop redirecting users to the Hong Kong site and comply with Chinese restrictions.

Probably as a result of the public row with Google, the State Council Information Office for the first time released its own white paper in June 2010, addressing the country's Internet policy. It warned foreigners, as well as local nationals, to respect China's laws and regulations. The government also reiterated its firm control over Web postings and its stance in censoring what it describes as unhealthy and damaging information. At the same time it acknowledged that the Internet is helping to promote the nation's economic and social development. (Internet-related industries are generating more than $100 billion in annual revenue.)

The white paper marked the first time China has publicly linked Internet control to an issue of Chinese sovereignty, elevating it to a national policy level. But the document was also about social stability, a major priority. The country's leaders are concerned that illicit information likely to create unrest will be disseminated online. (Facebook, YouTube, and Twitter are also subject to censorship in China.)

The details are quite clear in the white paper. It forbids organizations and individuals to produce, duplicate, announce, or disseminate illicit information that may endanger state security; divulge state secrets; subvert state power or jeopardize national unification; damage state honor and interest; instigate ethnic hatred; jeopardize state religious policy; propagate heretical or superstitious ideas; spread rumors; disrupt social order and stability; disseminate obscenity, pornography, gambling, violence, brutality, and terror or abet crime; humiliate or slander others; trespass on the lawful rights and interests of others.

Part of the government's rationale for its restrictions, of course, is that about a third of China's online users are under eighteen. Not surprisingly, one major concern is the pornography—much of it brutal—that is endemic on the Internet. Still, for Western readers accustomed to freedom of speech and individual rights, the contents of the white paper represent a level of government control that is probably hard to accept. To fully understand its purpose, however, readers need to understand how Chinese leaders regard the Internet as well as the country's particular history and culture.

To Chinese leaders, the rise of the Internet is a paradoxical issue. It is like a family faced with a precocious child—smart but often difficult to control. And political leaders are like parents trying their best not to let their child grow up to be a rebellious teenager, one who will disturb the stability of the family and cause problems in the neighborhood.

There is still another analogy to family life. Connecting with friends is one of the most important reasons people visit social networking websites, which are also becoming interactive platforms for creating, exchanging, and sharing ideas. The high proportion of young online users—growing up in a digital world that benefited from China's economic reforms and opening-up policies—are also from the generation born after China adopted the one-child-per-family policy. They are seeking friendship and social engagement to compensate for an often lonely childhood.

As long as netizens stay away from outright condemnation of the government and subjects relating to Tibet, Taiwan, and others the central government may deem inflammatory, people are generally free to share views and ideas online. Contrary to a lot of media and online coverage in the West, communication between citizens is quite open and information about almost every facet of daily life—from stock market share prices to cultural and entertainment news—is readily available.

With the increasingly widespread use of the Internet, especially by young people—60 percent of Internet users in China are under thirty—more and more diverse information, much of it never available before, is now potentially a keystroke away. This is why Beijing has set up a firewall to manage certain types of information that might create social instability or destabilize a region, or even the entire country. Government officials know the Internet played a role in incidents of civil disobedience over the past few years. The bloody ethnic riots in the western region of Xinjiang in July 2009, for example, were seen by Beijing as having been fueled by the microblogging site Twitter.

At the same time, the Internet can also be a tool to stoke the fires of nationalism. For example, when reports about the dispute between China and Japan over the Daioyu Islands were widely disseminated via the Internet—Japanese Coast Guard vessels apparently videotaped the incident, and these images were leaked online—this resulted in mass demonstrations in some cities. The governments of both China and Japan were concerned that old nationalist wounds would be reopened.

At the time, I remember receiving an e-mail circulating across the country advocating a full-scale boycott on Japanese products, arguing that if the Chinese population stopped buying these products for a month, thousands of Japanese companies would be financially burdened. There are no Japanese cars and television sets in South Korea, the argument continued, so why must China have them? (Of course, South Korea does not buy from the Japanese in part because of historical animosities between the countries and in large part because Korea produces these products itself.) This is an example of the power of the Internet and why China's leaders feel it is sometimes necessary to manage it.

It follows that Beijing will censor discussions relating to sensitive issues, among them the touchy issues of Tibet and Taiwan. Open opposition to the government is also forbidden. This may in part be related to the Chinese culture of respecting authority, as opposed to the West's belief that political opposition is good because it provides checks and balances. In Chinese culture, no one is allowed to criticize the leaders, because respect and dignity are considered sacrosanct. (Compare this to the widespread jokes and insults thrown at American political leaders, even presidents, which are encouraged by claims of freedom of speech and individual rights.)

I fully realize why many in the West would find it difficult to understand China's position on some of these issues. At the same time, Westerners need to see that—aside from certain sensitive issues—there is actually considerable Internet freedom in China. As a nation, it will have to deal with the benefits and challenges of new technology. China will certainly continue to evolve and manage its progress and transparency on a gradual basis. As I have suggested, however, the progress will be cautious. China is feeling the stones as it crosses the river.

Looking Ahead

I would like to close this chapter by mentioning an article that appeared in the *Wall Street Journal* late in 2010, along with a subsequent letter to the editor.

In the article, Bret Stephens, who is the paper's foreign affairs columnist and deputy editorial page editor, said, "Our time is supposed to be one of China's unstoppable rise and America's inevitable decline. Don't believe it. History is littered with the wreckage of regimes that thought they could create 'consensus' by suffocating dissent and steal intellectual innovation they could not generate on their own. China's bid to do just that merely compounds political error with historical ignorance."

Next day, in a letter to the editors, Dallas Weaver (someone I do not know and have been unsuccessful in tracking down) wrote, "When I visited China 25 years ago, it was clear that members of the Chinese Academy of Sciences fully understood that the West has dominated this planet for the last three centuries because of superior technology and its applications and not because of religion, philosophy or culture. China has been acting on this understanding ever since. The Chinese Government's first step was to increase the number and quality of the country's

STEM education: science, technology, engineering and mathematics. Chinese universities are graduating many times the number of scientists and engineers than we are. Almost all top positions in China's government are staffed by people with far more STEM knowledge than our corresponding political and bureaucratic classes. We in contrast, have been training our best and our brightest to be lawyers and bankers." The letter went on to say that China is investing heavily in R&D as I previously indicated. Weaver then commented further, "Of course, China doesn't have our political freedom. They do have a different kind of freedom, however: the freedom to actually build and create something . . . We creatively litigate while China creates, innovates and builds."[8]

9

WINDS OF CHANGE

CHINA'S DRIVE FOR ALTERNATIVE
ENERGY IS GAINING WORLDWIDE
ATTENTION AND RESPECT

In 2009 I went on an ocean cruise that left Buenos Aires and sailed around Cape Horn and up the coast of Chile to Santiago. This region boasts about having more glaciers than Alaska, so we were anxious to get a closer look. We took small boats to within a few hundred yards of several majestic glaciers before we had a surprise. Large chunks of ice were dropping into the ocean—a dramatic result of global warming.

Later, I read about other signs of this phenomenon in an Associated Press article published in the *South China Morning Post*. One of the warning signals included ticks carrying Lyme disease, which had been reported as far north as Sweden and Canada (countries thought to be too cold for these ticks to survive). Scientists were also concerned about malaria-transmitting mosquitoes found in South Korea, Papua New Guinea, and other regions formerly thought to be not warm enough for them. The giant Humboldt squid, which can destroy entire fish populations, had seldom been seen north of California, but now it was being spotted off Alaska. And bark beetles are spreading quickly through conifer forests, where temperatures are no longer cold enough to kill them off. The damage done by these insects is devastating forests across North America and increasing the risk of fire.[1]

Closer to my home, the temperature of the Yellow Sea, which lies between mainland China and South Korea, has risen as much as 1.7 °C (3 °F) during the past twenty-five years. As a result, more and more jellyfish are present in the water. These pests not only reduce the fish population, some species can actually spoil an entire catch if the fish come into contact with their venom. (The largest variety, known as Nomura, is wreaking havoc on the Japanese fishing industry.)

Although experts differ on the cause of the problem, most informed readers accept that the world needs to address climate change and other equally serious environmental issues. If the average temperature of the planet was to rise three or four degrees, for example, the results would be disastrous. Land cover would change dramatically. Polar ice caps would melt and raise sea levels, causing widespread flooding. People all over the world would be displaced because of altered seacoasts, loss of forests, and spreading deserts. These scenarios are not as far-fetched as some might suggest. As we witness the extraordinary flooding in Pakistan and Australia and the droughts in China in recent years, it is hard to ignore the calamities caused by extreme weather. International policies on global warming that are practical and integrated have now become essential.

Everybody's Business

But one of the difficulties is the global nature of the problem. The pollution caused by a country on one continent can have a major effect on countries halfway around the world. Equally challenging is the issue of developing nations, and particularly those (like China) that are going through a major shift in their level of industrialization. How can we come to a common understanding on the real environmental issues, and who can guide us to the solutions?

According to Lord Anthony Giddens, the renowned British sociologist and emeritus professor at the London School of Economics, three groups of people are involved in the discussion of climate change. The skeptics, who include many U.S. Republican politicians, say the claim that global warming is caused by human activities is unproven, or at least exaggerated. A second group is made up of those who support the orthodox position of the UN's Intergovernmental Panel on Climate Change (IPCC). These people (and the group includes most IPCC researchers and experts) want to bring together as much scientific evidence as possible to support the conclusion that climate change is indeed caused by human activities.

A third group involved in these worldwide discussions include the radicals who believe the scenario is apocalyptic. They say climate change is a far more urgent crisis than mainstream experts acknowledge. They believe the Earth is a living organism that will react violently to global warming, resulting in altered weather patterns around the world, which could produce changes as extreme as an ice age. (This is a very brief summary of Lord Giddens's ideas, of course; for more information, see his 2009 book, *The Politics of Climate Change*.)[2]

China's Role

China is caught in the middle of this debate, although its leaders are less concerned on a daily basis with international debates than with national concerns. (The more pressing issues are always growth and sustainability.) China continues to rely heavily on coal to support its economic growth, a reality that must change. Beijing, for example, is so polluted that often one cannot see across the road. Shanghai is not much better. Not surprisingly, China now burns half the coal used globally each year. Until enough clean and renewable energy projects kick in, China has no choice but to continue to use coal to fuel its economic growth.

The irony is that as developed countries close or limit the construction of coal-fired power plants, a number of the ports in Canada, Australia, Indonesia, Columbia, and South Africa are busy shipping coal to China. The United States has also been shipping coal to China via Vancouver or Prince Rupert, Canada (currently the only northwest ports with coal-handling capacity), and more recently it has been searching for port facilities in the state of Washington because new mines are being planned in the Rockies and the Pacific Northwest. Traditionally, coal is burned near where it is mined, especially thermal (steaming) coal used for heat and electricity. But China's appetite, at three billion tons a year, has necessitated long-distance supply chains, because the country's own domestic supplies tend to be low grade and riddled with impurities. It is more efficient to import, and ultimately the carbon footprint from cleaner coal will be smaller.

China is often regarded as being among the world's biggest polluters. The 2010 CO_2 *Emissions from Energy Use Index*, published by the U.K.-based global risk management consultancy Maplecroft.NET Limited, says China is the largest emitter of CO_2, even though it is ranked twenty-sixth on the index. Such statistics, of course, require interpretation. China's huge population makes its per capita emissions lower than countries such as the United Arab Emirates, Australia, the United States, and Canada. In fact, if every one of China's 1.3 billion citizens was associated with the same amount of CO_2 emissions as an American citizen, the country's total emissions would probably equal those of the entire world. Instead, China's emissions are a third less than those of America.[3]

China's high carbon emissions reflect its current stage of industrialization, because China is still considered a developing country with the potential for huge economic growth. Its reliance on coal as a major source of fuel contributes to the pollution problem, as do the growing numbers of cars and household appliances acquired by Chinese citizens as they make the transition from poverty to middle-class status. Still, China's president, Hu Jintao, has called for an ambitious target: cutting emissions per unit of economic output by 40 percent to 50 percent of 2005 levels by 2020.

This is one of many important steps China is taking to create what may soon become the world's leading low-carbon economy. I know that sounds unlikely, if not impossible, but consider the facts. In a report issued by the Climate Group, an international environmental NGO, China spent $12 billion in 2007 in absolute dollars invested on renewable energy. This means the country ranked second in the world only to Germany, which spent $14 billion in the same year. (China has likely since surpassed Germany in dollars invested.) The same report noted China's fuel efficiency standards for cars, which are 40 percent higher than those in the United States. For ethanol, China is already among the top three producers in the world. And this feat can be accomplished by using marginal land in the country—an area, in fact, that is half the size of the United Kingdom.

Meanwhile, an overview on China published by the not-for-profit National Center for Sustainable Development in Washington, D.C., concluded, "China has made significant progress in practically every low carbon economic sector in recent years and has already become a leader in a number of critical renewable energy markets. The evidence gathered suggests that China not only has the potential to become one of the largest forces in low carbon development, but that in various industries and according to several key metrics, China is already leading, generating jobs and profits along the way."

Other encouraging news came in October 2010 from the "Vivid Economics" report, produced by the Climate Institute, an Australian think tank. It named China as the world leader in clean energy efforts. According to this report, China is second only to Britain in the value of incentives it is providing for wind and solar power efforts to cut pollution from coal-powered electricity generation.

For the past five years, China has been quietly accomplishing these goals through a methodical, carefully planned strategy on the part of its political leaders. Their enormous task has been to engage the country's citizens as well as businesses, at home and abroad. Both government and business are influencing ordinary citizens to move away from the most polluting products and practices. For example, policies such as taxes on vehicles with large engines, mandatory energy efficiency standards, and prominent green-labeling of appliances all act as a kind of behavioral modification for China's population.

At the same time, various regulatory tools, subsidies, and investment incentives are being put in place to guide businesses to achieve the same goals. For example, in the northeastern industrial city of Shenyang, in Liaoning Province, building codes have been changed to require ground-source heat pumps for new buildings, and government subsidies are now available for the installation of solar panels. Meanwhile, in an effort to attract alternative industries to the steel town of Xinyu in Jiangxi Province, the city offered 200 million yuan ($30 million) in credit guarantees to LDK Solar, a producer of technology used in the manufacturing of solar panels. In 2007, LDK Solar attracted international attention when it was listed on the New York Stock Exchange. Now this firm and nine other solar suppliers have set up shop in Xinyu, which is today a leading home to solar and wind turbine manufacturers. China is now second only to the United States in wind power capacity.

I was on the Silk Road recently and saw many of the wind farms that lie next to the highways in the remote western hinterland. China's wind turbine manufacturing industry became the largest in the world in a mere four years. Three Chinese companies—Sinovel Wind, Goldwind Science and Technology, and Dongfang Electric—are among the top ten global companies in this field. China expects to produce 230 gigawatts of wind power capacity by the year 2020. To put this in perspective, that figure is equivalent to thirteen times the power capacity of the Three Gorges Dam. This wind power could, in fact, replace roughly two hundred coal-fired power generating plants. China is also one of the largest producers of solar photovoltaics (the technology used to convert solar radiation into electricity), accounting for 40 percent of worldwide needs. Leading companies in this field include Suntech, Bading Yingli, and JingAo Solar. All these facts are well documented in the "China World Power Outlook 2010," a report produced in cooperation with Greenpeace and the Global Wind Energy Council.

Some Chinese companies are now also expanding overseas. For example, Goldwind Science and Technology has established an operation in the United States despite the dim market prospects for wind turbine manufacturers. The U.S. market leader in this sector, General Electric, reported a sharp drop in third-quarter turbine sales in 2010 versus a year ago. Even now, the U.S. market is not an all-American affair because Vestas of Denmark, Siemens of Germany, and Mitsubishi of Japan are all there. But Chinese companies such as Goldwind can play a patient game because they are backed by the Chinese government in the form of low-interest loans (e.g., $6 billion from the China Development Bank) and they raised nearly $1 billion in an IPO in Hong Kong. Curiously, the Obama administration is investigating whether China has violated WTO rules in subsidizing its clean-energy industry. In the meantime, Goldwind is creating jobs in America.

CNOOC, China's largest offshore oil producer, recently announced that "new energy"—a term referring to nontraditional technologies such as solar, wind, and biomass energy—will account for 40–50 percent of the company's total energy production over the next five years (2011–15). Fu Chengyu, chairman of CNOOC, said wind power will account for 20–30 percent of the firm's total energy production during this period. CNOOC will also increase the use of liquefied natural gas, which produces less pollution and is regarded as a cleaner energy resource than oil or coal. Under pressure from the central government, CNOOC has constructed four natural gas terminals in coastal cities with six more to follow.

As CNOOC and other firms know, the real action in China today is in renewable energy. In its twelfth Five-Year Plan, released in March 2011, the central government has initiated a transition to become a low-carbon economy and society. Its goals of cutting greenhouse gas emissions by 40–50 percent and supporting 15 percent of its energy consumption from renewable sources by 2020 send clear signals: the government realizes the seriousness of the problem, and a major shift in mindset is occurring among the leadership.

Even greater evidence of Beijing's commitment came in June 2010 when Zhang Xiaoqiang, vice chairman of China's National Development and Reform Commission, gave an interview in London to address this 15 percent goal. "We can be sure we will exceed the 15 percent target," he said. "We will reach at least 18 percent. Personally, I think we could reach the target of having renewables provide 20 percent of total energy consumption."

China's long-term plan is to have renewable energy reach one-third of the country's total power capacity of 1,600 gigawatts by 2020. The actual breakdown by energy source would be as follows: hydro (300 gigawatts), wind (150 gigawatts), biomass (30 gigawatts), and solar (20 gigawatts). China, of course, benefits from the powerful will of the government to make this revolution happen, as well as an abundance of capital and a massive market. For example, in 2009, investment in this sector was $34.6 billion, compared to $18.6 billion in the United States.

Total renewable power capacity in China reached 226 gigawatts in 2009—more than one-quarter of the total installed power capacity

of 860 gigawatts. Hydro makes up the bulk of this capacity, at
197 gigawatts, followed by wind (25.8 gigawatts), biomass (3.2
gigawatts), and grid-connected solar power (0.4 gigawatts).[4] Late
in 2010, Astroenergy announced it would be building the world's
largest photovoltaic system at the Hangzhou East Railway Station
in Zhejiang, an eastern coastal province of China. Scheduled to
be ready by the end of 2011, the solar panels will cover 148,000
square meters and generate more than 9.8 million kWh annually.
When it begins operating, the system will replace 3,277 tons of
coal and reduce CO_2 emissions by 8,095 tons.[5]

There are other examples of China's progress in the environmental sector. In the eastern city of Suzhou, on the lower reaches
of the Yangtze River in Jiangsu Province, the state-owned China
Energy Conservation and Environment Investment Corporation is
in the process of building the country's first "environmental and
high-tech industrial park" to focus on environmental R&D. And
the national government has provided 47 million yuan ($7 mil-
lion) in financial subsidies to six construction projects in the port
of Qingdao in Shandong Province that are classified as national
demonstration projects for the use of marine energy.

All these signs of progress bring to mind the proverb attributed
to fifth-century BC philosopher Lao Zi, who offered this thoughtful advice: "A journey of a thousand li [miles] starts with a single
step." What many Westerners may not appreciate is the difficulty
of that thousand-mile journey. China's rush into industrialization
and a new urban economy have meant a corresponding increase
in the need for power. But it takes enormous amounts of *water* to
create power. In 2009, roughly 160 trillion gallons of water were
available for all uses in China. Nearly 25 percent of this water
was needed for industrial purposes, and most of it (roughly 80
percent) was destined for cooling technology in coal-burning gen-
erators at 550 power plants.

At the current rate of consumption, power-related water needs
will rise to 70 trillion gallons by the year 2030. And there simply is not enough water to meet that need—not if China wishes
to provide sufficient food for its population from local farmers.
China will have to become an ever-increasing importer of foods
from abroad. Ironically, the country might have to import rice,

for example, because China cannot afford to use scarce and expensive water to grow a food staple that is readily available and cheap to import. With sufficient water, the country could easily be self-sufficient in terms of agricultural products. Water is actually becoming the most precious commodity for both the United States and China.

The U.S. Role

Meanwhile, it is worth looking at how the United States has been responding to the energy question. In 2005, Congress directed the Department of the Interior to approve enough wind, solar, and other renewable projects on public land to produce ten thousand megawatts by 2015. This figure represents enough power to heat, cool, and light five million homes. However, very little progress has been made on this initiative. Until mid-2010, the Department of the Interior had approved 73,000 oil and gas leases—but only one offshore wind project and not a single major solar project.

Under the Democrats and President Barack Obama, however, some hopeful signs have been evident. He declared in 2009 that no industry has greater potential to create jobs than the clean energy sector. As part of his Recovery Act he unveiled an ambitious energy plan that awarded $2.3 billion in January 2010 for new clean-tech manufacturing projects to be created across the United States. His government approved six large-scale solar power projects on public land—five in California and one in Nevada. Together, these will provide enough power for two million homes. Ken Salazar, the interior secretary, gave final approval to America's first commercial offshore wind farm, which is scheduled to be built off the coast of Massachusetts. A group of companies, including Google, has also announced plans to build an underwater transmission system to carry wind-generated power from public land along the Atlantic coast to cities on that same seaboard.

The same year, unwilling to rely solely on the government, seven leading CEOs set up the American Energy Innovation Council: Chad Holliday, chairman of the Bank of America and former CEO of DuPont; Microsoft's Bill Gates; Jeff Immelt, CEO of General Electric; Tim Solso, CEO of power giant Cummins; Ursula Burns,

CEO of Xerox; Norm Augustine, former CEO of Lockheed Martin; and John Doerr, a partner at the Silicon Valley-based private equity firm Kleiner Perkins Caufield & Byers. Together they hope to encourage the government to further boost R&D investment in clean energy and create technology clusters so research universities, government labs, and the private sector will be able to work together. The council firmly believes that America needs a long-term energy strategy to move toward a low-carbon economy while still creating more jobs.[6]

However, with many states in America having budget concerns, a push to speed up renewable energy development may meet heavy resistance. The new Congress, which now includes many more conservatives, will probably be disinclined to take concrete action on global warming. In fact, they might start holding hearings to question the Environmental Protection Agency and international climate science. For the foreseeable future, it may be impossible for the U.S. Congress to pass national cap-and-trade policies. Meanwhile, global greenhouse gas emissions continue to climb.

In the meantime, it has been more than a decade since the United States Senate failed to ratify the Kyoto Protocol on Climate Change, which was negotiated during the Clinton administration. Since then it has seemed inevitable that any treaty designed to cut greenhouse gas emissions would probably be a lost cause. There is an enormous gulf between the developed countries led by the United States and the developing countries led by China on how to address global warming issues. The 2009 Climate Conference held in Copenhagen demonstrated how the Kyoto approach might well have design flaws that could lead to a dead end.

In a November 2010 article in the *New York Times*, James P. Rubin, assistant secretary of state in the Bureau of Public Affairs during the Clinton years and now an adjunct professor at Columbia's School of International and Public Affairs, summed up the problem. "If treaties can't make it through the [U.S.] Senate anymore," he suggested, "maybe we should do away with them." In the case of climate change, he added, "In recent years negotiators have continued to pursue international climate agreements but with the understanding that adherence would occur through domestic energy legislation that the rest of the world could then examine and assess."[7]

Work for the Future

I am personally skeptical about how these global summits (with more than 190 countries participating and America and China at loggerheads) will yield any major breakthroughs. For the sake of future generations, however, we cannot afford to abandon them. Let us hope the gathering in Cancun, Mexico, held in the late fall of 2010 leads to some progress on issues such as finance, technological transfer, deforestation prevention, and skill building in poorer countries as well as the legal status of any future treaties. I am inclined to believe that a modest agreement among the participating nations would be better than no agreement at all.

However, I would be surprised to see any deal on emission controls because of the level of mistrust between America and China—with each side coming from an apparent position of self-interest. I feel strongly that binding commitments on the part of the United States would be the only way to secure formal and lasting commitments from China. The international gathering scheduled for late 2011 in South Africa may be an opportunity for both nations to make further progress. In the meantime, it is not helpful to read about the "Buy American" provision that Congress enacted into law in January 2011 for U.S. Defense Department purchases of solar panels. The law was written in a way that particularly prevents the United States from buying Chinese-made solar panels. The wording was carefully crafted to help comply with the free trade rules of the WTO.

My strongest sense about environmental issues is that we need innovative thinking at *all* levels of government, and we need to show how "green thinking" can also be green in the sense of financially rewarding. If alternative energy can create jobs, it will be embraced more quickly. For example, the World Challenge global competition initiated by the BBC, *Newsweek*, and Shell in 2005 and now in its sixth year demonstrated how remote mountain communities in the Philippines could use hydraulic systems to push water uphill to needy villages. Along the way, the power system created employment opportunities.

Similarly, the Husk Power System in the state of Bihar (India) came up with a clever way to turn waste into power. Rice husks are usually left to rot in the fields, and this releases methane gas into the atmosphere. By burning the husks and trapping the gases, the system can power engines that turn alternators and create electricity. Whole villages now have electric power for the first time—and the planet has proportionally less methane contributing to global warming.[8]

Transportation using only human energy, of course, is a simple way to tackle carbon dioxide problems. The Hangzhou Bicycle Rental Company, which was initially financed locally but is now a state-owned business, has developed a rental business in Hangzhou, the capital of Zhejiang Province. It is modeled after the successful Vélib' bike rental program in Paris. With fifty thousand bikes and two thousand rental stations in Hangzhou, the company is helping develop similar programs in other Chinese cities.[9]

Global climate change threatens to increase the frequency and severity of natural disasters—with significant security implications that defense ministries on both sides are beginning to realize and acknowledge. Militaries on both sides have the necessary logistical structures to cooperate in providing disaster relief and humanitarian assistance. The U.S. and China can be new partners because neither on its own can confront the human dislocation and competition for resources caused by environmental degradation. A U.S.-China climate security pact could draw on the science and technology of both countries. This would help improve mutual trust and understanding.

In the end and for the foreseeable future, party politics may get in the way in America, and a better prospect could be a Europe-China joint initiative to move global initiatives forward. But my preference would be for cooperative efforts with America. If more international gatherings could focus on creative and cooperative alternatives—whether large-scale or small—rather than mere shoptalk or haggling over political postures, I believe we might see greater progress toward a genuinely greener world.

THE DREAM TEAM

CHINA AND AMERICA MUST PUT
POLITICS ASIDE AND WORK TOGETHER
FOR THE BENEFIT OF THE PLANET AND
FOR FUTURE GENERATIONS

On Christmas Day 2010, a friend sent me a philosophical end-of-the-year e-mail that included some thought-provoking statistics. If we were to fit the world's population into a village of one hundred people, there would be fifty-seven Asians, thirty-five people of European descent, and eight Africans and people of other origins. Of these, 80 percent would be living in poverty (on $10/day), and 50 percent would suffer from hunger and malnutrition.

Thinking about this, I wondered why nations are spending so much on defense activities—from military drills and exercises to arms races to regional wars—that do little for the common folk around the world. It is as though billions of dollars are being dropped into the ocean. What a waste.

Some Western observers have been concerned about China's own increased defense spending, but consider the facts. In 2010, the United States is estimated to have spent $636 billion, more than eight times China's $78 billion defense expenditure. Imagine, though, if the United States and China instead took the lead and rallied other countries to join them in cutting defense spending. These funds could be used to address poverty, starvation, disease, and climate change—all issues we must address for the sake of future generations. It is time we ended the obsession with weapons of mass destruction and focused instead on promoting world peace.

Countless articles and books have been written about the shift of power from West to East, many proclaiming that the twenty-first century belongs to China. Personally, I feel this may be far too simplistic. Being as familiar as I am with America, I would not write off that country just yet! Many more innovative leaders on a par with Steve Jobs, Bill Gates, and Sergey Brin will emerge to keep America in the forefront of creativity and innovation. Most Americans have been brought up to be competitive. All one has to do is attend an NFL or college football game to feel the spirit. The American Dream is still very much alive, but it is politics that appears to be in the way. The term *American Dream* probably has roots in the Great Depression, when historian James Truslow Adams defined it as the "dream of a land in which life should be better and richer and fuller for everyone with opportunity for each according to ability or achievement." This seems to be what the Chinese leaders are striving for—making a similar dream a reality for its huge population.

In the meantime, China still faces many challenges, despite the impressive macroeconomic numbers it has so far achieved. With close to half of its population in poverty, it is still a developing nation. The central government in Beijing is putting its focus on maintaining social stability by controlling inflation and balancing economic development across the country so the wealth gap among the haves and have-nots does not widen, causing social unrest. It is also promoting domestic consumption to increase imports and help the West regain its footing.

To further illustrate challenges faced by China, here's what Premier Wen Jiabao had to say when he chatted with netizens at Xinhua.net.cn early in 2011:[1]

- *On inflation:* I'm very familiar with the daily price of food and commodities such as meat, oil, eggs and vegetables because I check the price index daily. Please trust me, the man who pays great attention to prices every day won't allow prices to keep soaring out of control.

- *On housing:* I want to suggest to real estate developers:
  I haven't investigated the profits of every one of you, but
  I think you real estate developers, as members of society,
  should do your own bit for society. You should have
  morality running in your veins.

- *On wealth distribution:* We should not only make the
  cake of social wealth as big as possible, but also distribute
  the cake in a fair way and let everyone enjoy the fruits of
  reform and opening-up.

- *On anti-corruption:* No matter who they [the officials] are,
  no matter what senior positions they hold, as long as they
  break the law . . . they will all receive severe punishment.

- *On governance evaluation:* An official's performance and
  political achievements should be evaluated by whether
  the public are happy or not, dissatisfied or not, but not by
  how many high-rise buildings and projects he had been
  involved in.

For the first time, the central government has incorporated a whole chapter on enhancing "social governance" in its latest five-year plan (up to 2015). Chinese Leaders at the 2011 National People's Congress pledged to boost incomes of less wealthy citizens in line with the rate of the country's economic growth, and they called for companies to raise workers' wages so they match productivity gains. This may well be a reflection on growing concern over domestic instability and contagion from the unrest in the Middle East.

With widespread complaints over the lack of affordable housing (contributed partly by property speculation and partly by infla-tion), the central government will now spend close to $200 billion (1.3 trillion yuan) on subsidized housing, representing a two-thirds increase over 2010. Some ten million low-cost homes will be built in 2011, with a commitment to build 36 million over the next five years. Other measures taken during 2010 to rein in runaway property prices included raising minimum down-payment levels, establishing punishment for speculators, and experimenting with real estate taxes in major cities. China has also raised interest rates three times since October 2010, to try to keep down inflation.

This is, however, a balancing act, because investment in real estate construction accounts for a growing share of China's GDP—roughly

10 percent now. Allocation of land for low-cost housing versus supply available in the commercial sector must be carefully managed because the implications for demand on steel, cement, copper, and other materials are part of the overall equation.

The other issue revolves around food supply and soaring food prices. In the past several decades, we have witnessed rapid urbanization and industrialization, but agriculture has lagged behind. Consequently, about 18 percent of the central government's 2011 budget will go to agriculture and farmers. Safeguarding food security for the 1.3 billion population has become a top priority. A severe drought that hit the south of China in 2009, for example, left millions of rural people lacking clean water and affected the productivity of farmland.

Another drought during the winter in 2010 in the wheat-growing provinces revealed a need to improve outdated irrigation systems. The government has promised to spend 4 trillion yuan ($615 billion) in the next ten years to rebuild water conservancy projects and improve water-use efficiency. The next five-year plan indicates that close to 3 million hectares of farmland will be more efficiently irrigated by 2015.

Unavoidable Interconnection

Today, both globalization and communications (driven by technology) have resulted in China and America being interconnected and dependent on each other as never before. But the U.S.-China relationship will continue to be a roller-coaster ride, mainly because of differences in the countries' respective political and financial systems, as I have outlined in earlier chapters.

As part of a series of articles about China's next five-year plan, State Councillor Dai Bingguo, who has emerged as among the most respected figures in Chinese foreign policy in the Hu Jintao administration, was quoted in the South *China Morning Post* as saying, "The notion that China wants to replace the United States and dominate the world is a myth. China's so-called strategic intent is not as complicated and abysmal as some people have imagined—as if we have some secret agenda and ambitions." Councillor Dai went on to reiterate that China's strategy could be encapsulated by the catchphrase "peaceful development," meaning a focus on China's own development while cooperating peacefully with other nations.[2]

Reinforcing this conciliatory message, President Hu said in his 2009 end-of-year address that all countries should join China to help create "a beautiful future of world peace and development."[3] And in his 2010 address, he said: "I believe, as long as the people from all countries make efforts hand in hand, the world will have a better future and the welfare of the people from all countries will be improved."[4]

China may in the not-so-distant future be the largest economy in the world. Some analysts are even predicting (after the recent financial crisis) that this could happen in a decade's time. Nevertheless, if we measure China on a per-capita income basis, it will continue to be a developing country for the foreseeable future. The other important factor to note is that China's civilization goes back thousands of years and is very different from that of the West. Most people in America and the West tend to assume that as China modernizes, it will become more like the West. Perhaps in terms of daily material things such as cars and mobile phones it may, but culturally China will remain very different. China should, therefore, not be judged solely on Western values and standards.

I should also point out that China's notion toward the issue of race is also very different from that of the West. Because over 90 percent of the population belong to the group known as Han Chinese, they tend to stick together—which, in my view, is why we see Chinatowns in many of the major cities around the world. My Chinese friends in Hawaii, for instance, are far more traditional than Chinese in Hong Kong. Chinese are, therefore, loyal to their race, whereas Americans and Europeans are far more patriotic to their country. This is why Beijing is trying to cultivate nationalism.

Despite moving more and more toward a market economy, the state is still everywhere. To the Chinese, the state is not only viewed as a member of the family but is revered as the patriarch. This means that the state holds considerable legitimacy in the minds of the Chinese people. This also partly explains why the sovereignty issue is often not negotiable.

Recent disputes over the Diaoyu Islands with Japan and claims over islands in the South China Sea may have given the impression that China is becoming "assertive"—a word increasingly being used by Western journalists when I sense they really want to say "aggressive." Chinese leaders are trying hard to change this perception. President Hu's state visit to the United States in January 2011 indicated that China's intention is to help with global recovery while making sure that China's social stability can be maintained through continued economic growth. (See Appendix B.)

Tensions in the Korean Peninsula have also raised concerns in both China and the United States. China called for the resumption of the six-party talks—originally created in 2003 to find a peaceful resolution to security concerns about North Korea's nuclear weapons program. But the United States and Japan, along with South Korea, were not supportive of this initiative, calling it a public relations exercise. So, having conducted a massive military exercise in the Sea of Japan with U.S. involvement, South Korea continued to conduct drills near the disputed North-South divide. This type of provocation seems to me not only counterproductive but highly risky, especially when the North Korean regime has proven to be so volatile and unpredictable.

Meanwhile, the United States accused China of not taking a tougher stance reining in North Korea. What readers need to understand is that China has a policy of not interfering with other nations' affairs. As a result, while officials would do their best quietly and behind the scenes as mediators, China would not use aggressive arm-twisting techniques. Instead they would hope that the nations involved—South Korea, the United States, Russia, and Japan—would join forces with them to help resolve the friction. Contrary to the Western belief that China is uninterested in a united Korea, officials have repeatedly stated that China supports a unified Korean peninsula. In fact, this was even reported among the exchange of diplomatic correspondence between the United States and China that was disclosed by whistleblower website WikiLeaks in 2010.

One-sided bashing of China at every opportunity does not help the global economic recovery nor promote world peace.

I was, therefore, surprised and saddened to read an article in a December issue of the *Honolulu Star-Advertiser* titled, "Season Brings Reminder of U.S. Reliance on China." That title appears inoffensive, but the content was otherwise. Here is a partial quote from the article: "The creepy thing: China is not our friend, but it's become our keeper. America's Christmas trees groan with ornaments made in the country that lets North Korea threaten our troops and Asian friends. China supports the regime of the bizarre Kim Jong-il and his son, bent on strutting the world stage as a nuclear menace. China could close down the North Korean freak show tomorrow but it won't because that would create a unified Korea allied with the U.S. China does not want us to have strong ties in Asia."[5]

It is indeed unfortunate that the author, Froma Harrop, who ranks twentieth among the top hundred syndicated columnists for total reader reach and fourteenth based on average circulation, would exhibit this kind of attitude. Her twice-a-week column appears in two hundred newspapers across America and, even more surprising, she has a reputation as being a liberal. (Imagine what the right-wing pundits might say.) No wonder the American public has a distorted view of relations between China and the United States.

When it comes to foreign policy, China needs to understand that Western rhetoric is driven by domestic politics. Having played such a dominant global role for so long, it is difficult for America to change its mindset to share the world stage with a fast-rising economic competitor. China's ascent can be seen as a rebalancing of world powers so that wealth and quality of life can be more evenly distributed. With more Chinese students studying in U.S. educational institutions and more American and European students going to China to further their studies and learn the language, the next generation will no doubt have a deeper understanding of each other's cultures and develop more trust between the two countries. Deng Xiaoping once said. "When our thousands of Chinese students abroad return home, you will see how China will transform itself." Increased two-way tourist traffic will also help.

Building Bridges

There are times when it seems that cuisine has been one of the best bridges between the two cultures. Everyone knows how much Americans like Chinese food. The first Chinese restaurant in America opened in San Francisco in 1849, and today the number of Chinese restaurants is greater than the number of McDonald's, Burger King, and KFC outlets combined. That's why national chains such as P. F. Chang's China Bistro, Panda Express, and Manchu Wok are so successful. But don't forget that iconic American chains such as Kentucky Fried Chicken, McDonald's, and Pizza Hut have achieved record revenues in China as well.

As for business relations, on the whole American and Chinese businesspeople get along well and respect each other's skill sets, especially as more and more of them gain experience with each other's cultural habits. As more Americans do business in China, they have become more familiar with the often complex way business is conducted in China. But, at the same time, a rising Chinese business class has become inclined to soften the rigid rules surrounding Chinese tradition and etiquette to accommodate U.S. visitors.

In the larger corporate sphere, there have for years been examples of partnerships between Chinese and foreign companies, but today some of the world's industrial giants are going further—integrating parts of their global operations into joint venture deals so together the companies can do business around the world. For example, in late 2010 General Electric created an equal partnership with military jet manufacturer Aviation Industry Corporation of China. The deal gives GE access to a Chinese government project that will compete with Boeing and Airbus in the civilian aircraft market. What would have been impossible to imagine even two decades ago was GE agreeing to include in the venture all its existing worldwide business in nonmilitary avionics.

Another example is the General Motors Sail. Launched in 2010, the Sail was the first car created in China by a Sino-foreign joint venture between GM and China's SAIC Motor Corporation. The car has been well received and plans are being made to export it to other emerging markets. GM sold 2.35 million cars in China in 2010. Coda Holdings, a California start-up that uses Chinese manufacturing and battery technology, is expected to start selling its first all-electric car in the United States in the second half of 2011. Fosun International, with an asset base of around $15 billion, has recently decided to convert itself from an industrial conglomerate to an investment holding company in partnership with Prudential Financial of the United States. "Our strategy is very clear," Guo Guangchang, Fosun's chairman, said at a press conference in Beijing. "In five to ten years' time, we want to transform our business to be more like that of Warren Buffett's Berkshire Hathaway Inc." In June 2010, for instance, Fosun bought a 7 percent stake in the French leisure group, Club Méditerranée, which Fosun will help expand in China. These kinds of joint efforts symbolize a new spirit of cooperation among Western and Chinese corporations.

I am, therefore, glad to see that President Hu and President Obama both stressed the importance of partnership during President Hu's state visit to Washington in January 2011. President Hu said, "China and the United States share broad common interests and important common responsibilities." He added that both countries should adopt a long-term perspective, seek common ground while reserving differences, and work together to achieve sustained, sound, and steady development of relations. He further stressed that "China and the United States should respect each other's choice of development path and each other's core interests." President Obama, in his welcome speech, said, "We have an enormous stake in each other's success . . . Even as our nations compete in some areas, we can cooperate in others. What Deng Xiaoping said long ago remains true today: there are still great possibilities for cooperation between our two countries." He also said that President Hu's visit served to lay the foundation for deeper prosperity between the two countries in decades to come, ending his remarks in Chinese: *huanying* (welcome).[6]

These are all nice words expressed within the context of diplomacy. However, in reality, it may not be a simple matter to avoid conflict. China and the United States have different political systems and cultures. They are at different stages of economic development and exist an ocean apart from each other. Some of their respective ideologies and values are also different. America is a melting pot of many ethnic backgrounds, while China is predominantly Han Chinese. Some political analysts in both China and the West point to history in that competition, because world supremacy has inevitably led to either a cold war or a hot one—and there are worries that America and China will follow a similar path.

Today, there are certainly issues on which America and China disagree:

- How to solve the trade and investment imbalance
- How human rights issues should be dealt with in each country
- How to resolve the Taiwan question, as well as problems with North Korea, Iran, Sudan, Myanmar, and now the Middle East
- Which role each country should take in East Asia
- The respective degree of responsibility for climate change.

America will no doubt continue to push China to become democratic (as defined by the United States). And China will no doubt move very gradually on this front, because any misstep could erase some of the success in bringing millions out of poverty. Meanwhile, China would like to see the United States manage its own economic and financial affairs better and refrain from lecturing other nations. China itself has shown pragmatic accommodation on many fronts, preferring to focus on its domestic challenges. The only exception is safeguarding its territorial integrity.

Although historically the issue of supremacy has often focused on military capabilities, competition today centers more on international commerce and the mastery of innovative ideas and knowledge. With globalization, nations around the world are increasingly interdependent. In integrating itself into the global economy, China has benefited enormously from this interconnected environment, capturing on one hand its fair share of foreign direct investment and becoming the world's largest exporter on the other. This success, however, has also created many domestic challenges, which I have addressed in different chapters and which the next Five Year Plan will cover.

In his speech at the U.S.-China Business Council gathering during his state visit, President Hu again reiterated that China's economic rise was not achieved at the cost of U.S. jobs, and its military modernization poses no threat to other countries. China is not interested in engaging in an arms race and will never seek to dominate or pursue an expansionist policy. Instead, China's demand for imports has generated millions of jobs, and its rise would benefit America and the rest of the world. China's inexpensive exports have saved American consumers an estimated $600 billion in the past decade. China welcomes other countries that wish to participate in its development. As a sign of this good will, in the run-up to the summit there were reports that U.S. and Chinese companies signed close to $45 billion in U.S. export deals.

Media and Message

I think the perceived conflicts between the two countries have been largely created by the Western media's one-sided reporting, which in turn affects the behavior of Western officials and politicians. One answer is a stronger Chinese media, but language is obviously a factor in China's drive to develop a more global reach for its media. (Beijing has recently stepped up its funding in an effort to better promote its image around the world.) However, it will be a long time before a Chinese media outlet can match the influence of the likes of CNN, CNBC, BBC, the *Wall Street Journal*, the *International Herald Tribune*, the *New York Times*, the *Financial Times*, and the *Economist*.

I was encouraged by an article by Zbigniew Brzezinski, national security adviser in Jimmy Carter's administration, published in the *International Herald Tribune* in January 2011. Remarking on President Hu's upcoming visit to the United States, Brzezinski recalled an equally historic visit made by president Deng Xiaoping more than three decades earlier. At that time, during an era of Soviet expansionism, Deng's visit led to a cooperative China-U.S. opposition to the Soviet Union's global ambitions. But this new diplomatic relationship also kick-started China's economic transformation, which is so impressive today.

Calling for a forthright discussion of the differences as well as similarities that characterize the two countries, Brzezinski wrote: "They should declare their commitment to the concept that the American-Chinese partnership should have a wider mission than national self-interest. That partnership should be guided by the moral imperatives of the 21st century's unprecedented global interdependence."[7]

Henry A. Kissinger, who served as national security adviser and secretary of state under Presidents Richard Nixon and Gerald Ford (and was instrumental in the opening of U.S. relations with China), wrote an article titled "The U.S. and China Don't Need a Cold War" in *International Herald Tribune*, also in January 2011. His concluding remarks: "The aim should be to create a tradition of respect and cooperation so that the successors of leaders meeting now continue to see it in their interest to build an emerging world order as a joint enterprise."[8]

A Course of Action

What do America and China each need to do to foster a more balanced relationship so they can become a Dream Team capable of tackling the pressing challenges facing all of humanity? Here are ten suggestions I would respectfully present to each side:

For America:

- Accept the fact that China is a different country. Try to understand the complexity of the Chinese society and respect its development priorities. Consider altering the prevailing mindset to build trust and achieve a genuine partnership.

- Understand the preoccupation that Chinese leaders have with social order and harmony. The increase in military spending is more for defense than aggression toward other nations.

- Become more pragmatic and less political on foreign policies, while maintaining values and ideals. Reducing provocative public rhetoric would be helpful.

- Scale back defense spending and spend more on maintaining a leading role in innovation. Create more knowledge-based industries, which in turn will create jobs.

- Encourage businesses, especially large corporations, to sacrifice earnings for a few years to fund R&D and create jobs.
- Provide government incentives to grow small- and medium-sized private companies so they can do more hiring.
- Refocus education toward science and mathematics, and retrain workers for new innovative industries. Major reskilling is urgently needed.
- Relax exports of as many technologies as possible to help rebalance trade.
- Allow more Chinese acquisitions of U.S. assets, because these investments will help create jobs.
- Develop financial policies based on a global perspective rather than self-interest. The quantitative easing approach, for example, was counterproductive.

For China:

- Develop a more secure profile on the world stage. Be more statesmanlike when responding to perceived international provocation. This will help improve Western perceptions of China.
- Allow more freedom of expression within China, and continue to push for more balanced economic development across the country.
- Continue to develop policies to fight inflation and enhance domestic consumption. Stepping up improvement in healthcare and pension schemes will enable citizens to spend more on a variety of goods and services. Introduce policies to build a larger middle class by reducing the overall tax structure and resolving the housing issue.
- Promote innovation while maintaining a role as the factory of the world.
- Continue to revalue the yuan, albeit on a gradual basis. Raising interest rates should also be considered to better protect the value of people's savings.
- Continue to help emerging nations through appropriate trade, investment, and aid policies.

- Import more from the United States and Europe to help with the global economic recovery.

- Ensure a level playing field for multinationals and local companies alike.

- Strengthen education at all levels, in particular in the areas of management and technology.

- Continue to develop the renewable energy sector, irrespective of stalled global coordination.

In the end, genuine mutual trust between China and the West—particularly the United States—is the answer not only to world peace but to the formation of a Dream Team capable of tackling climate change in earnest, promoting better healthcare, and eradicating poverty and hunger in many parts of the world. We owe this to future generations, who will attach far less importance to our current differences than does the current generation. Indeed, they will challenge us if we fail to meet our obligations on a global level. This is the time for East and West to join together to face that challenge through more regular dialogue. We must respect each other's domestic challenges and work on equal terms in the interest of all.

AFTERWORD

Perhaps inspired by the uprisings in the Arab world, an anonymous writer posted a provocative online message on Boxun.com on February 20, 2011. He urged people in China to gather, stroll, watch, or just pass by at designated sites in selected cities across China every Sunday. Perhaps the writer believed this would draw large crowds and gain even greater media attention. I imagine this attempt to destabilize China was probably instigated by Chinese dissidents, many of whom are now refugees in the West. (Boxun.com is a Chinese-language news-site based in the United States.)

The resulting crowds were small, and there were relatively few incidents that were newsworthy. Some arrests were made, and some websites were blocked. A few foreign journalists were even supposedly being closely watched. But the reasons were obvious. The Central Government, in the midst of the ongoing National People's Congress proceedings, was not willing to take any chances that social unrest might take a foothold in China. The security forces were out in force after this online "invitation." But instead of using pepper spray and water cannons, these government employees used street-cleaning water trucks to keep people from gathering at the designated sites. And regardless of the motivation of the online writers, their goal was not reached.

Unfortunately, these instigators have probably not had the opportunity to witness first-hand what is happening in China. They will not have seen the successful developments and progress being made in recent decades as millions were lifted out of poverty and given a chance to enjoy more freedom. Positive change can be seen everywhere. The Central Government has clearly made a commitment to keep improving the livelihood of people, especially in the rural west, and to spread the recent economic and social successes more evenly across all sectors of the society.

Am I surprised that calls for a "jasmine revolution" are not succeeding in China? Not really. Any calls for "taking to the streets" will likely not succeed for one simple reason. Since the time of Mao, China has not been ruled by single-minded dictators such as Egypt's Hosni Mubarak, Libya's Muammar Gaddafi, or Tunisia's Ben Ali. China is being managed by a stable and institutionalized collective leadership with a ten-year tenure. Their mandate is simply to get things done. The Central Authority is composed of well-educated and well-intentioned leaders, and they are doing their best to minimize corruption and make the country an influential power on the world stage. Unlike those in the Arab world, young people in China today can see the opportunities for individual advancement resulting from China's economic growth. In fact, Chinese people of all ages are in the process of regaining their pride.

Although the nascent "uprising" was quelled, it did not go unnoticed by those in power. Following repeated online calls for the pro-democracy rallies, China's top legislator, Wu Banggu, addressed the situation. In his report at the National People's Congress, he indicated that China would not adopt Western-style democracy. His message was clear: "We must maintain the correct political orientation and never waiver on key issues of principle such as our fundamental system of the State." He added that relaxing the Party's grip on power would undermine stability and risk domestic strife. Banggu reacted strongly and negatively to a call for the separation of powers. Moving toward Western-style democracy was simply not an option, he said. China was not going to adopt a system of multiple parties holding office in rotation. Instead, there would be a continuation of executive, legislative, and judicial powers operating under one central leadership.

In my opinion, any political reform going forward, if it happens at all, will be gradual at best. There will be debate in the West, of course, over the wisdom of this stance. But it is hard to deny that the one-party rule and collective leadership model appears to be serving China well. Even though financial analysts predict a slowdown in growth in the country's economy in the next few years, this is to be expected. China's leadership is simply trying to prevent the economy from becoming a runaway train. Overall, I still believe the current system is functioning well and serving the best interests of everyone in China.

Meanwhile, there are continuing signs that the world at large is paying considerable attention to China. Gary Locke's nomination to be the next U.S. Ambassador to China has been hailed by most media articles and commentators as an astute White House move. This is the first time that a cabinet-level official has been appointed to this post, which signals the importance being placed by the Obama Administration on the U.S.-China relationship (and presumably "giving China face"). Locke has past experience in leading trade delegations to China, which strengthens the appointment. In fact, he sat in on most meetings involving U.S.-China matters, so he has solid experience in bilateral negotiations. The press noted that he is a first-generation Chinese-American (his father was from Guangdong and his mother from Hong Kong). And Locke knows some of the top Chinese leaders personally.

On the negative side, some commentators say this appointment is all about identity politics. President Obama gets to curry favor with the Chinese by sending them an American with a Chinese ethnic background as his envoy. At the same time, Obama can now curry favor with the American business community by appointing a CEO (probably from one of the Fortune 500 companies) to become the next Secretary of Commerce.

There has been a suggestion that Gary Locke is not a Putonghua (Mandarin) speaker, because the dialect he picked up from his parents when he was young would be either Cantonese or Toisan. Critics also say he apparently does not read or write Chinese because he grew up in America. Personally, I do not know whether there is any truth to these rumors. I have only met Locke once, and that was in Seattle when he was Governor of Washington State. He was amicable and approachable—personality traits that should serve him well in Beijing. On balance, we should welcome Locke's appointment wholeheartedly, because any development that will foster better U.S.-China relationship going forward deserves our full support.

It is my hope that Locke will be supportive on issues that involve China on delicate international matters. For example, the recent politics relating to the top post at the International Monetary Authority (IMF) suggest that the West is still trying to cling to power while ignoring the economic shift from West to East. The process does not appear to be carried out "on equal terms." At the time of this writing, the leading candidate from France was making an effort to lobby the BRIC countries (Brazil, Russia, India, and China) because funding for the IMF will increasingly be coming from these sources. Western countries (including Locke's nation) need to deal with one of the most dramatic new economic realities. China is becoming the banker to the world.

Unfortunately, this issue was not much in evidence at the G8 summit in Deauville in May, 2011. The international gathering did not come up with any breakthrough solutions for rebalancing the global economy. This is not surprising when one looks at the membership (the United States, the United Kingdom, France, Germany, Italy, Canada, Russia, and Japan). With the shift in economic power, the G8 is clearly no longer relevant without the participation of China, India, and Brazil.

We need to admit the obvious. The G8 created in 1975 belongs to the old world order. As a result of the financial crisis in 1997/98, the G20 was created in 1999. In my view, this group is far too large to be really effective. A smaller group—based more on their economic ability to provide necessary leadership to address the global imbalance—should now be considered. If the G8 was replaced with a G9, and it included the United States, China, Japan, Germany, the United Kingdom, Brazil, France, Russia, and India as members, the balance of international power might be better addressed.

As countries all over the world come to terms with global issues, we need to meet and discuss our common concerns. And what is even more important, we must do it on *equal terms* and on mutual trust as expressed by U.S. Navy Admiral and Chairman of the Joint Chiefs of Staff Mike Mullen in his July 27, 2011 article in the *International Herald Tribune's* Opinion page entitled "A Step toward trust with China."[1]

APPENDIX A

CHINA'S CURRENT LEADERSHIP

These are the members of the Politburo Standing Committee of the Communist Party of China:

1. Hu Jintao (age sixty-nine): General Secretary of the CPC, President of the PRC, Chairman of the Central Military Commission

2. Wu Bangguo (age seventy): Chairman of the Standing Committee of the National People's Congress

3. Wen Jiabao (age sixty-nine): Premier of the State Council of the People's Republic of China

4. Jia Qinglin (age seventy-one): Chairman of the National Committee of the Chinese People's Political Consultative Conference

5. Li Changchun (age sixty-seven): "Propaganda Chief"

6. Xi Jinping (age fifty-eight): Top-ranked Secretary of CPC Secretariat, Vice President of the People's Republic of China, Vice Chairman of the Central Military Commission

7. Li Keqiang (age fifty-six): First-ranked Vice Premier of the State Council of the People's Republic of China

8. He Guoqiang (age sixty-eight): Secretary of Central Commission for Discipline Inspection

9. Zhou Yongkang (age sixty-nine): Secretary of Political and Legislative Affairs Committee

Note: The leaders' ages are given as of early 2011.

APPENDIX B

CHINA-U.S. JOINT STATEMENT

WASHINGTON, Jan. 19 (Xinhua): China and the United States on Wednesday issued a joint statement, which covers a range of issues such as strengthening bilateral relations, addressing regional and global challenges, building a comprehensive and mutually beneficial economic partnership, and cooperating on climate change, energy and the environment. Following is the full text of the joint statement:

China-U.S. Joint Statement January 19, 2011, Washington

1.   At the invitation of President Barack Obama of the United States of America, President Hu Jintao of the People's Republic of China is paying a state visit to the United States of America on January 18–21, 2011. During his visit, President Hu also met with Vice President Joseph Biden, will meet with U.S. Congressional leadership, and will visit Chicago.

2.   The two Presidents reviewed the progress made in the relationship since President Obama's November 2009 state visit to China and reaffirmed their commitment to building a positive, cooperative and comprehensive China-U.S. relationship for the 21st century, which serves the interests of the Chinese and American peoples and of the global community. The two sides

Source: http://news.xinhuanet.com/english2010/china/2011-01/20/c_13698492_2.htm

reaffirmed that the three Joint Communiqués issued by China and the United States laid the political foundation for the relationship and will continue to guide the development of China-U.S. relations. The two sides reaffirmed respect for each other's sovereignty and territorial integrity. The Presidents further reaffirmed their commitment to the November 2009 China-U.S. Joint Statement.

3.   China and the United States are committed to work together to build a cooperative partnership based on mutual respect and mutual benefit in order to promote the common interests of both countries and to address the 21st century's opportunities and challenges. China and the United States are actively cooperating on a wide range of security, economic, social, energy, and environmental issues which require deeper bilateral engagement and coordination. The two leaders agreed that broader and deeper collaboration with international partners and institutions is required to develop and implement sustainable solutions and to promote peace, stability, prosperity, and the well-being of peoples throughout the world.

Strengthening China-U.S. Relations

4.   Recognizing the importance of the common challenges that they face together, China and the United States decided to continue working toward a partnership that advances common interests, addresses shared concerns, and highlights international responsibilities. The two leaders recognize that the relationship between China and the United States is both vital and complex. China and the United States have set an example of positive and cooperative relations between countries, despite different political systems, historical and cultural backgrounds, and levels of economic development. The two sides agreed to work further to nurture and deepen bilateral strategic trust to enhance their relations. They reiterated the importance of deepening dialogue aimed at expanding practical cooperation and affirmed the need to work together to address areas of disagreement, expand common ground, and strengthen coordination on a range of issues.

5.   The United States reiterated that it welcomes a strong, prosperous and successful China that plays a greater role in world

affairs. China welcomes the United States as an Asia-Pacific nation that contributes to peace, stability and prosperity in the region. Working together, both leaders support efforts to build a more stable, peaceful, and prosperous Asia-Pacific region for the 21st century.

6.   Both sides underscored the importance of the Taiwan issue in China-U.S. relations. The Chinese side emphasized that the Taiwan issue concerns China's sovereignty and territorial integrity, and expressed the hope that the U.S. side will honor its relevant commitments and appreciate and support the Chinese side's position on this issue. The U.S. side stated that the United States follows its one-China policy and abides by the principles of the three China-U.S. Joint Communiqués. The United States applauded the Economic Cooperation Framework Agreement between the two sides of the Taiwan Strait and welcomed the new lines of communications developing between them. The United States supports the peaceful development of relations across the Taiwan Strait and looks forward to efforts by both sides to increase dialogues and interactions in economic, political, and other fields, and to develop more positive and stable cross-Strait relations.

7.   China and the United States reiterated their commitment to the promotion and protection of human rights, even as they continue to have significant differences on these issues. The United States stressed that the promotion of human rights and democracy is an important part of its foreign policy. China stressed that there should be no interference in any country's internal affairs. China and the United States underscored that each country and its people have the right to choose their own path, and all countries should respect each other's choice of a development model. Addressing differences on human rights in a spirit of equality and mutual respect, as well as promoting and protecting human rights consistent with international instruments, the two sides agreed to hold the next round of the China-U.S. Human Rights Dialogue before the third round of the Strategic and Economic Dialogue (S&ED).

8.   China and the United States agreed to hold the next round of the resumed Legal Experts Dialogue before the next Human Rights Dialogue convenes. China and the United States further agreed to strengthen cooperation in the field of law and exchanges

on the rule of law. China and the United States are actively exploring exchanges and discussions on the increasing role of women in society.

9.   China and the United States affirmed that a healthy, stable and reliable military-to-military relationship is an essential part of President Hu's and President Obama's shared vision for a positive, cooperative, and comprehensive China-U.S. relationship. Both sides agreed on the need for enhanced and substantive dialogue and communication at all levels: to reduce misunderstanding, misperception, and miscalculation; to foster greater understanding and expand mutual interest; and to promote the healthy, stable, and reliable development of the military-to-military relationship. Both sides noted the successful visit of Secretary of Defense Robert Gates to China earlier this month, and that the United States welcomes Chief of the PLA General Staff General Chen Bingde to the United States in the first half of 2011. Both sides reaffirmed that the Defense Consultative Talks, the Defense Policy Coordination Talks, and the Military Maritime Consultative Agreement will remain important channels of communication in the future. Both sides will work to execute the seven priority areas for developing military-to-military relations as agreed to by Secretary Gates and General Xu Caihou, Vice Chairman of the Central Military Commission in October 2009.

10.   China and the United States agreed to take specific actions to deepen dialogue and exchanges in the field of space. The United States invited a Chinese delegation to visit NASA headquarters and other appropriate NASA facilities in 2011 to reciprocate for the productive visit of the U.S. NASA Administrator to China in 2010. The two sides agreed to continue discussions on opportunities for practical future cooperation in the space arena, based on principles of transparency, reciprocity, and mutual benefit.

11.   China and the United States acknowledged the accomplishments under the bilateral Agreement on Cooperation in Science and Technology, one of the longest-standing bilateral agreements between the two countries, and welcomed the signing of its extension. China and the United States will continue to cooperate in such

diverse areas as agriculture, health, energy, environment, fisheries, student exchanges, and technological innovation in order to advance mutual well-being.

12.   China and the United States welcomed progress by the China-U.S. Joint Liaison Group on Law Enforcement Cooperation (JLG) to strengthen law enforcement cooperation across a range of issues, including counterterrorism. China and the United States also agreed to enhance joint efforts to combat corruption through bilateral and other means.

Promoting High-Level Exchanges

13.   The two sides agreed that high-level exchanges are indispensable to strong China-U.S. relations, and that close, frequent, and in-depth dialogue is important to advance bilateral relations and international peace and development. In this spirit, both Presidents look forward to meeting again in the coming year, including in the state of Hawaii for the U.S.-hosted 2011 Asia-Pacific Economic Cooperation (APEC) Leaders' meeting. China welcomed Vice President Biden for a visit in 2011. The United States welcomed a subsequent visit by Vice President Xi Jinping.

14.   The two sides praised the S&ED as a key mechanism for coordination between the two governments, and agreed to hold the third round of the S&ED in Washington, D.C., in May 2011. The S&ED has played an important role in helping build trust and confidence between the two countries. The two sides also agreed to hold the second meeting of the High-Level Consultation on People-to-People Exchange in the United States in the spring of 2011, and the 22nd meeting of the China-U.S. Joint Commission on Commerce and Trade (JCCT) in China in the second half of 2011. The two sides agreed to maintain close communication between the foreign ministers of the two countries through mutual visits, meetings, and other means.

15.   The two sides emphasized the importance of continued interaction between their legislatures, including institutionalized exchanges between the National People's Congress of China and the U.S. Senate and House of Representatives.

Addressing Regional and Global Challenges

16.   The two sides believe that China and the United States have a common interest in promoting peace and security in the Asia-Pacific region and beyond, and agreed to enhance communication and coordination to address pressing regional and global challenges. The two sides undertake to act to protect the global environment and to work in concert on global issues to help safeguard and promote the sustainable development of all countries and peoples. Specifically, China and the United States agreed to advance cooperation to: counter violent extremism; prevent the proliferation of nuclear weapons, other weapons of mass destruction, and their means of delivery; strengthen nuclear security; eliminate infectious disease and hunger; end extreme poverty; respond effectively to the challenge of climate change; counter piracy; prevent and mitigate disasters; address cyber-security; fight transnational crime; and combat trafficking in persons. In coordination with other parties, China and the United States will endeavor to increase cooperation to address common concerns and promote shared interests.

17.   China and the United States underlined their commitment to the eventual realization of a world without nuclear weapons and the need to strengthen the international nuclear non-proliferation regime to address the threats of nuclear proliferation and nuclear terrorism. In this regard, both sides support early entry into force of the Comprehensive Nuclear Test Ban Treaty (CTBT), reaffirmed their support for the early commencement of negotiations on a Fissile Material Cutoff Treaty in the Conference on Disarmament, and agreed to work together to reach these goals. The two sides also noted their deepening cooperation on nuclear security following the Washington Nuclear Security Summit and signed a Memorandum of Understanding that will help establish a Center of Excellence on Nuclear Security in China.

18.   China and the United States agreed on the critical importance of maintaining peace and stability on the Korean Peninsula as underscored by the Joint Statement of September 19, 2005 and relevant UN Security Council Resolutions. Both sides expressed concern over heightened tensions on the Peninsula triggered by

recent developments. The two sides noted their continuing efforts to cooperate closely on matters concerning the Peninsula. China and the United States emphasized the importance of an improvement in North-South relations and agreed that sincere and constructive inter-Korean dialogue is an essential step. Agreeing on the crucial importance of denuclearization of the Peninsula in order to preserve peace and stability in Northeast Asia, China and the United States reiterated the need for concrete and effective steps to achieve the goal of denuclearization and for full implementation of the other commitments made in the September 19, 2005 Joint Statement of the Six-Party Talks. In this context, China and the United States expressed concern regarding the DPRK's claimed uranium enrichment program. Both sides oppose all activities inconsistent with the 2005 Joint Statement and relevant international obligations and commitments. The two sides called for the necessary steps that would allow for early resumption of the Six-Party Talks process to address this and other relevant issues.

19.   On the Iranian nuclear issue, China and the United States reiterated their commitment to seeking a comprehensive and long-term solution that would restore international confidence in the exclusively peaceful nature of Iran's nuclear program. Both sides agreed that Iran has the right to peaceful uses of nuclear energy under the Non-Proliferation Treaty and that Iran should fulfill its due international obligations under that treaty. Both sides called for full implementation of all relevant UN Security Council Resolutions. China and the United States welcomed and will actively participate in the P5+1 process with Iran, and stressed the importance of all parties—including Iran—committing to a constructive dialogue process.

20.   Regarding Sudan, China and the United States agreed to fully support the North-South peace process, including full and effective implementation of Sudan's Comprehensive Peace Agreement. The two sides stressed the need for all sides to respect the result of a free, fair, and transparent referendum. Both China and the United States expressed concern on the Darfur issue and believed that further, substantive progress should be made in the political process in Darfur to promote the early, comprehensive,

and appropriate solution to this issue. Both China and the United States have a continuing interest in the maintenance of peace and stability in the wider region.

21. The two sides agreed to enhance communication and coordination in the Asia-Pacific region in a spirit of mutual respect and cooperation, and to work together with other Asia-Pacific countries, including through multilateral institutions, to promote peace, stability, and prosperity.

Building a Comprehensive and Mutually Beneficial Economic Partnership

22. President Hu and President Obama recognized the vital importance of working together to build a cooperative economic partnership of mutual respect and mutual benefit to both countries and to the global economy. The two leaders agreed to promote comprehensive economic cooperation, and will further develop a framework of comprehensive economic cooperation, relying on existing mechanisms, by the third round of the S&ED in May, based on the main elements outlined below:

23. The two sides agreed to strengthen macroeconomic communication and cooperation, in support of strong, sustainable and balanced growth in the United States, China and the global economy.

- The United States will focus on reducing its medium-term federal deficit and ensuring long-term fiscal sustainability, and will maintain vigilance against excess volatility in exchange rates. The Federal Reserve has taken important steps in recent years to increase the clarity of its communications regarding its outlook and longer-run objectives.

- China will intensify efforts to expand domestic demand, to promote private investment in the service sector, and to give greater play to the fundamental role of the market in resource allocation. China will continue to promote RMB exchange rate reform, enhance RMB exchange rate flexibility, and promote the transformation of its economic development model.

- Both sides agree to continue to pursue forward-looking monetary policies with due regards to the ramifications of those policies for the international economy.

The two sides affirmed support for efforts by European leaders to reinforce market stability and promote sustainable, long-term growth.

24.   The two countries, recognizing the importance of open trade and investment in fostering economic growth, job creation, innovation, and prosperity, affirmed their commitment to take further steps to liberalize global trade and investment, and to oppose trade and investment protectionism. The two sides also agreed to work proactively to resolve bilateral trade and investment disputes in a constructive, cooperative, and mutually beneficial manner.

25.   The two leaders emphasized their strong commitment to direct their negotiators to engage in across-the-board negotiations to promptly bring the WTO Doha Development Round to a successful, ambitious, comprehensive, and balanced conclusion, consistent with the mandate of the Doha Development Round and built on the progress already achieved. The two sides agreed that engagement between our representatives must intensify and expand in order to complete the end game.

26.   The two leaders agreed on the importance of achieving a more balanced trade relationship, and spoke highly of the progress made on this front, including at the recent 21st Meeting of the Joint Commission on Commerce and Trade in Washington, D.C.

27.   China will continue to strengthen its efforts to protect IPR, including by conducting audits to ensure that government agencies at all levels use legitimate software and by publishing the auditing results as required by China's law. China will not link its innovation policies to the provision of government procurement preferences. The United States welcomed China's agreement to submit a robust, second revised offer to the WTO Government Procurement Committee before the Committee's final meeting in 2011, which will include sub-central entities.

28.   The two leaders acknowledged the importance of fostering open, fair, and transparent investment environments to their

domestic economies and to the global economy and reaffirmed their commitment to the ongoing Bilateral Investment Treaty (BIT) negotiations, recognizing that a successful BIT negotiation would support an open global economy by facilitating and protecting investment, and enhancing transparency and predictability for investors of both countries. China welcomed the United States' commitment to consult through the JCCT in a cooperative manner to work towards China's Market Economy Status in an expeditious manner. China welcomed discussion between the two sides on the ongoing reform of the U.S. export control system, and its potential implications for U.S. exports to its major trading partners, including China, consistent with U.S. national security interests.

29.   The two sides further acknowledged the deep and robust nature of the commercial relationship, including the contracts concluded at this visit, and welcomed the mutual economic benefits resulting from the relationship.

30.   The two sides agreed to continue working to make concrete progress on the bilateral economic relationship through the upcoming S&ED and the JCCT process.

31.   China and the United States recognized the potential for their firms to play a positive role in the infrastructure development in each country and agreed to strengthen cooperation in this area.

32.   The two countries committed to deepen bilateral and multilateral cooperation on financial sector investment and regulation, and support open environments for investment in financial services and cross-border portfolio investment, consistent with prudential and national security requirements. The United States is committed to ensuring that the GSEs have sufficient capital and the ability to meet their financial obligations.

33.   China and the United States agree that currencies in the SDR basket should only be those that are heavily used in international trade and financial transactions. In that regard, the United States supports China's efforts over time to promote inclusion of the RMB in the SDR basket.

34.   The two countries pledged to work together to strengthen the global financial system and reform the international financial architecture. The two sides will continue their strong cooperation

to strengthen the legitimacy and improve the effectiveness of the International Monetary Fund and Multilateral Development Banks (MDBs). The two sides will jointly promote efforts of the international community to assist developing countries, in particular the Least Developed Countries to achieve the Millennium Development Goals (MDGs). The two sides will also, in partnership with the Multilateral Development Banks, explore cooperation that supports global poverty reduction and development, and regional integration including in Africa, to contribute to inclusive and sustainable economic growth.

35. The two countries reiterated their support for the G-20 Framework for Strong, Sustainable and Balanced Growth and reaffirmed their commitments made in the Seoul Summit Declaration, including using the full range of policies to strengthen the global recovery and to reduce excessive imbalances and maintain current account imbalances at sustainable levels. The two sides support a bigger role for the G-20 in international economic and financial affairs, and pledged to strengthen communication and coordination to follow through on the commitments of the G-20 summits and push for positive outcomes at the Cannes Summit.

Cooperating on Climate Change, Energy and the Environment

36. The two sides view climate change and energy security as two of the greatest challenges of our time. China and the United States agreed to continue their close consultations on action to address climate change, coordinate to achieve energy security for our peoples and the world, build on existing clean energy cooperation, ensure open markets, promote mutually beneficial investment in climate friendly energy, encourage clean energy, and facilitate advanced clean energy technology development.

37. Both sides applauded the progress made in clean energy and energy security since the launch of the China-U.S. Clean Energy Research Center, Renewable Energy Partnership, China-U.S. Joint Statement on Energy Security Cooperation, and Energy Cooperation Program (ECP). Both sides reaffirmed their ongoing exchanges on energy policy and cooperation on oil, natural gas (including shale gas), civilian nuclear energy, wind and solar energy, smart grid,

advanced bio-fuels, clean coal, energy efficiency, electric vehicles and clean energy technology standards.

38.   The two sides commended the progress made since the launch of the China-U.S. Ten Year Framework on Energy and Environment Cooperation (TYF) in 2008. They agreed to further strengthen practical cooperation under the TYF, carry out action plans in the priority areas of water, air, transportation, electricity, protected areas, wetlands, and energy efficiency, engage in policy dialogues, and implement the EcoPartnerships program. China and the United States were also pleased to announce two new EcoPartnerships. The two sides welcomed local governments, enterprises, and research institutes of the two countries to participate in the TYF, and jointly explore innovative models for China-U.S. energy and environment cooperation. The two sides welcomed the cooperation projects and activities which will be carried out in 2011 under the TYF.

39.   The two sides welcomed the Cancun Agreements and believed that it is important that efforts to address climate change also advance economic and social development. Working together and with other countries, the two sides agreed to actively promote the comprehensive, effective, and sustained implementation of the United Nations Framework Convention on Climate Change, including the implementation of the Cancun agreements and support efforts to achieve positive outcomes at this year's conference in South Africa.

Expanding People-to-People Exchanges

40.   China and the United States have long supported deeper and broader people-to-people ties as part of a larger effort to build a cooperative partnership based on mutual respect and mutual benefit. Both sides agreed to take concrete steps to enhance these people-to-people exchanges. Both sides noted with satisfaction the successful Expo 2010 in Shanghai, and the Chinese side complimented the United States on its USA Pavilion. The two sides announced the launch of a China-U.S. Governors Forum and decided to further support exchanges and cooperation at local levels in a variety of fields, including support for the expansion of

the sister province and city relationships. China and the United States also agreed to take concrete steps to strengthen dialogue and exchanges between their young people, particularly through the 100,000 Strong Initiative. The United States warmly welcomes more Chinese students in American educational institutions, and will continue to facilitate visa issuance for them. The two sides agreed to discuss ways of expanding cultural interaction, including exploring a China-U.S. cultural year event and other activities. The two sides underscored their commitment to further promoting and facilitating increased tourism. China and the United States agreed that all these activities help deepen understanding, trust, and cooperation.

Conclusion

41.   President Hu Jintao expressed his thanks to President Obama and the American people for their warm reception and hospitality during his visit. The two Presidents agreed that the visit has furthered China-U.S. relations, and both sides resolved to work together to build a cooperative partnership based on mutual respect and mutual benefit. The two Presidents shared a deep belief that a stronger China-U.S. relationship not only serves the fundamental interests of their respective peoples, but also benefits the entire Asia-Pacific region and the world.

GLOSSARY

ABB   A global leader in power and automation technologies—a Swiss-Swedish multinational.

AEIC   The American Energy Innovation Council was established by seven U.S. business leaders including Bill Gates and GE's Jeff Immelt to support R&D on clean energy technology.

ASEAN   The Association of Southeast Asian Nations is a geo-political and economic organization of ten countries formed in 1967—initially by Indonesia, Malaysia, the Philippines, Singapore, and Thailand. Later Brunei, Myanmar, Cambodia, Laos, and Vietnam were added.

ATRA   A chemotherapy drug used to treat acute promyelocytic leukemia (APL, APML).

BBC   The British Broadcasting Corporation is the state-owned public service broadcaster in the United Kingdom.

BCG   Boston Consulting Group.

BYD   BYD Automobile Company is a Chinese automobile manufacturer in Shenzhen; it is part of BYD, an innovative maker of rechargeable batteries.

CCP   Chinese Communist Party.

CCTV   China Central Television is the major state television broadcaster in mainland China.

CEO   Chief Executive Officer.

CFIUS   The U.S. Committee on Foreign Investment in the United States is the federal interagency body charged with reviewing any foreign investment that may have national security implications.

CMC   China's Central Military Commission.

CNBC   A satellite and cable television business news channel in the United States.

CNN   Cable News Network—a U.S. cable news channel founded in 1980 by Ted Turner.

COD   Collect on delivery.

COMAC   Commercial Aircraft Corporation of China is a Chinese aerospace manufacturer established in 2008.

CRI   China Radio International is one of two State-owned radio stations. The other is China National Radio (CNR).

C2C   Consumer-to-consumer transactions online.

danwei   *Danwei* is the word for *bureau* in Chinese (Putonghua, or Mandarin).

EMBA   Executive Master of Business Administration degree—meeting educational needs of executives while they work full time (classes usually carried out over weekends).

EU   The European Union is an economic and political union of member states in Europe.

FAW   China's first automobile manufacturer—also makes buses, trucks, and other vehicles.

G20   Group of twenty finance ministers and central bank governors from leading economies—comprising about 85 percent of world's GDP.

G8   A forum created by France in 1975 for governments of France, Germany, Italy, Japan, the United Kingdom, Canada, Russia, and the United States.

GDP   Gross domestic product; the term refers to the market value of all goods and services produced within a country in a given period.

GPS   Global Positioning System; a space-based global navigational satellite system that provides reliable direction and location.

hai gui   *Hai gui* is pinyin for "sea turtles"—slang for Chinese talents returning to China from overseas.

hexie shehui *Hexie shehui* is pinyin for "harmonious society."

HXMT Hard X-ray modulation telescope in a planned X-ray space observatory from China to be launched in 2012.

IATA International Air Transport Association—represents 230 airlines around the world.

IBM International Business Machines is an American multinational technology and consulting company.

IFC International Finance Corporation is a member of the World Bank that promotes sustainable private sector investment in developing countries.

IFF International Flavors and Fragrances, a company listed on New York Stock Exchange.

IMF The International Monetary Fund is the intergovernmental organization that oversees the global financial system by following the macroeconomic policies of its member countries—particularly those with an impact on exchange rate and the balance of payments.

IPCC The UN Intergovernmental Panel on Climate Change.

KFC Kentucky Fried Chicken—a fast food chain owned by Yum Brands.

KMT *Kuomingtang,* translated as the Chinese National Party, which was founded by Sun Yat-sen and subsequently led by Chiang Kai-shek. After their defeat by the Communist forces, Chiang and his followers retreated to Taiwan. Today, KMT in Taiwan is led by President Ma Ying-jeou.

LTE Long Term Evolution, a mobile network in Sweden.

LVMH A French holding company and world's leading luxury goods conglomerate. It is the parent company of some sixty sub-companies and brands.

MAC Middle-income and affluent consumers.

MBA Master of Business Administration degree.

MDGs Millennium Development Goals. A set of international goals framed by the United Nations and directed at developing countries.

NDRC   China's National Development and Reform Commission is a macroeconomic management agency under the State Council.

NGO   A nongovernmental organization is a legally constituted body created by a natural or legal person that operates independently from any government—it has no government status.

NPC   China's National People's Congress.

OECD   The Organization for Economic-Cooperation and Development is an international economic organization founded in 1961 to stimulate economic progress and world trade.

OEM   An original equipment manufacturer makes products and components that are purchased by a brand-owning company.

OOCL   Orient Overseas Container Line.

PAP   China's People's Armed Police.

PLA   China's People's Liberation Army.

PRC   People's Republic of China.

Putonghua   *Putonghua* is the pinyin rendering of the name of China's official language—Mandarin.

REIT   Real Estate Investment Trust—a structure designed to provide a similar structure for investment in real estate as mutual funds provide for investment in stocks.

RMB   *Renminbi* is the pinyin version of yuan—the term for China's currency. RMB or Renminbi can be used interchangeably with yuan.

SAIC   Shanghai Automotive Industry Corporation (not to be confused with SAIC, a Fortune 500 engineering group).

SDR   A special drawing right is a monetary unit of international reserve assets defined and maintained by the International Monetary Fund. The unit is not a currency but represents a potential claim on the currencies of the IMF members for which it may be exchanged as a form of balance of payments.

SOE   State-owned enterprise.

STEM   Science, technology, engineering, and mathematics (related to education).

UBS   A Swiss global financial services company.

Yin Yang   In Chinese philosophy, Yin Yang is normally used to describe how polar or seemingly contrary forces are interconnected and interdependent in the natural world and how they give rise to each other in turn.

YMCA   The Young Men's Christian Association is a worldwide organization established in London by Sir George Williams. Its goal is to put Christian principles into practice.

yuan   This is the base unit of today's Chinese currency; the term is used interchangeably with Renminbi.

YWCA   The Young Women's Christian Association is a global network of women leading social and economic change in countries worldwide.

NOTES

Introduction

1. May Chan, "Asia Overtakes Europe in Billionaire Table," *South China Morning Post*, March 11, 2011.
2. *China Daily*, "Price Soars as Top Flight Bird Heads to China," January 15, 2011.
3. Global Language Monitor, "Top News Stories of the Decade: The Rise of China Surpasses Iraq War and 9/11," December 9, 2009.
4. CNN GO (numerous authors), "The World's Greatest City: 50 Reasons Why Hong Kong Is No. 1," October 5, 2009; available online: www.cnngo.com/explorations/none/worlds-greatest-city-166098; access date: April 15, 2011.
5. Yang Cheng and Lin Qi, "Constructive Ties with China Hailed," *China Daily*, September 9, 2010.
6. Richard J. Leider and David A. Shapiro, *Repacking Your Bags: Lighten Your Load for the Rest of Your Life* (San Francisco: Berrett-Koehler, 2002).
7. Lam Kam Chuen, *The Feng Shui Handbook: How to Create a Healthier Living and Working Environment* (New York: Henry Holt, 1996).

Chapter 1

1. Orville Schell, "The Short March," *South China Morning Post*, September 25, 2009.

Chapter 2

1. Greg Torode and Ambrose Leung, "Tung Tells U.S. to Go Easy on Yellow Sea," *South China Morning Post,* September 19, 2010.
2. John Mearsheimer, "The Rise of China Will Not Be Peaceful at All," *The Australian*, November 18, 2005.

3. Chris Buckley, "Chinese Admiral Says U.S. Drill Courts Confrontation," Reuters, August 13, 2010.

4. M. Taylor Fravel, *Strong Borders, Secure Nation: Cooperation and Conflict in China's Territorial Disputes* (Princeton, NJ: Princeton University Press, 2008).

5. Michael Swaine, "The U.S.-China Spat at Sea," *Carnegie Endowment for International Peace—Foreign Policy*, March 11, 2009.

6. Eric C. Anderson, "China Matters, Now . . . An Open Letter to the President," *Huffington Post*, March 13, 2009.

7. Helene Cooper, "U.S. Toward China: View of a Sole Superpower," global edition of the *New York Times* in the *International Herald Tribune*, November 29, 2010.

8. "China Buys Spanish Bonds After Buying Portuguese Debt," *Guardian* (U.K.), January 13, 2011.

Chapter 3

1. "Candidates Using China as a Punchbag," *South China Morning Post*, October 11, 2010, quoting from the *New York Times*.

2. David D. Hale and Lyric Hughes Hale, "Reconsidering Revaluation," *Foreign Affairs*, January/February, 2008. Published by the Council on Foreign Relations.

3. "Chesapeake Energy Corporation and CNOOC Ltd announce Eagle Ford Shale Project Cooperation Agreement," *Killajoules Oil and Gas Sector News*, October 13, 2010.

4. "ConocoPhillips Completes Sale of Syncrude Stake to Sinopec," *Oil Voice*, June 27, 2010.

5. "Small Business Trends," Alibaba.com press release, August 27, 2010.

6. "The All-China Federation of Industry and Commerce 2011 Report," *China Daily*, February 9, 2011.

7. "Interview with Wu Jia Yuan, Chairman of Hubei Dengfeng Heat Exchange Co. Ltd.," *China Knowledge at Wharton*, February 3, 2010.

8. Barry Naughton, *The Chinese Economy: Transitions and Growth* (Cambridge, MA: MIT Press, January 2007).

9. The Commission of Experts on Reforms of the International Monetary and Financial System, Recommendations, United Nations General Assembly, March 19, 2009.

10. Jamil Anderlini, "China Wants to Oust Dollar as International Reserve Currency," *Financial Times*, March 24, 2009.

11. Patrick Jenkins, "China Lenders Eclipse U.S. Rivals," *Financial Times*, January 11, 2010.

Chapter 4

1. Sara Bongiorni, *A Year Without "Made in China"—One Family's True Life Adventure in the Global Economy* (Hoboken, NJ: Wiley, 2008).

2. David Barbosa, "Made in China Labels Don't Tell Whole Story," *New York Times*, February 8, 2006.

3. Yuqing Xing and Neal Detert, "How the iPhone Widens the United States Trade Deficit with the People's Republic of China," ADBI Working Paper 257, Tokyo: Asian Development Bank Institute, December 2010.

4. "The $6.50 Trade War," *Wall Street Journal*, Opinion Review and Outlook section, January 10, 2011.

5. "Obama Delivers Remarks at a Luncheon for Patty Murphy," *Washington Post,* August 17, 2010.

6. Jeffrey Sachs, *The End of Poverty* (New York: Penguin, 2005).

7. Stephen Roach, "The Silver Lining of Wage Increase," *China Daily*, July 27, 2010.

8. Leslie T. Chang, *Factory Girls: From Village to City in a Changing China* (New York: Spiegel & Grau, 2008).

Chapter 5

1. "Long Hated One-Child Rule May Be Eased in China," *USA Today*, April 24, 2010.

2. Yuval Atsmon et al., "2009 Annual Chinese Consumer Study, Part II: One China Many Markets," McKinsey Insights China, 2009.

3. Wang Fangqing, "Food Makers Catering to Local Tastes in China," Just Food website, March 11, 2010.

4. Jennifer Reingold, "Can P&G Make Money in Places Where People Earn $2 a Day?" *Fortune*, January 17, 2011.

5. Carry Huang, "Big-City Dwellers on a Long March to the Hills," *South China Morning Post,* May 17, 2010.

6. Jeff Walters et al., "The Keys to the Kingdom: Unlocking China's Consumer Power," Boston Consulting Group, March 2010.

7. "Meeting the Challenges of China's Growing Cities," *McKinsey Quarterly*, July 2008.

8. "China's Five Best New Cities for Business," *Fortune*, October 18, 2010.

Chapter 6

1. Mark Drajem and Rebecca Christie, "Geithner Warning on Yuan May Renew U.S.-China Tension (Update 3)," *Bloomberg News*, January 23, 2009.

Chapter 7

1. Joseph Nye, *Soft Power: The Means to Success in World Politics* (New York: Perseus Books, 2004).

2. Jeremy Paltiel, "Mencius and World Order Theories," *Chinese Journal of International Politics*, February 10, 2010.

3. "Hu Jintao Calls for Enhancing Soft Power of Chinese Culture," Xinhua News Agency, October 15, 2007.

4. Heng Yee Kuang, "Soft Power: Singapore Has What It Takes," *Straits Times*, July 3, 2010.

5. "China's Soft Power Set for Global Audience," *China Daily*, August 20, 2010.

6. Gary Jones, "Anna Wintour in Beijing," *Post Magazine, SCMP*, December 19, 2010.

7. "Milan Fashion Awaits Chinese Design Boom," Reuters, February 28, 2011.

8. Wang Qian, "Information Official: Nation Needs to Extend Soft Power," *China Daily*, September 15, 2010.

9. Derek Scissors, "China Global Investment Tracker 2011," Heritage Foundation, January 10, 2011.

10. Jessica Shepherd, "China's Top Universities Will Rival Oxbridge Says Yale President," *Guardian*, February 2, 2010.

11. Duan Yan, "The American Dream of the Chinese Rich," *China Daily*, August 6, 2010.

12. Joseph Nye, "The New Public Diplomacy," Project Syndicate, February 10, 2010.

13. Matthew Bewley, "Old Neighbors in a New World," *Harvard Political Review*, December 5, 2010.

Chapter 8

1. Ashlee Vance, "China Wrests Supercomputer Title from U.S.," *New York Times*, October 28, 2010.

2. David Martin and Jim Fitzgerald, "IBM's WATSON beats 'Jeopardy!' Champs Ken Jennings and Brad Rutter in First Public Test," Associated Press, January 13, 2011.

3. Fiona Tam, "Shenzhen's Electric Cabs Blaze Trail for China's Car Industry," *South China Morning Post*, May 24, 2010.

4. Stefan Wagstyl, "Is Global Brand Innovation Essential for Success in Emerging Economies?" *Financial Times*, January 6, 2011.

5. Alice Yan, "Traditional Medicine and Findings from West Led to Breakthrough," *South China Morning Post*, February 22, 2011.

6. "Chinese Netizens Create Cyber Words to Make Language More 'Geilivable,'" *People's Daily*, December 25, 2010.

7. Boston Consulting Group, "China's Digital Generation 2.0," May 2010.

8. Bret Stephens, "China and the Next American Century," *Wall Street Journal*, December 21, 2010. This article was followed next day in the Letters to the Editor column by "China Creates While America Litigates," a letter signed Dallas Weaver.

Chapter 9

1. Associated Press, "Other pests riding the wave of climate change," *South China Morning Post*, November 17, 2009.

2. Anthony Giddens, *The Politics of Climate Change* (Cambridge, U.K.: Polity Press, 2009).

3. Maplecroft Ltd. Global Risk Management Consultancy, "The 2010 CO_2 Emission from Energy Use Index," November 17, 2010.

4. Eric Martinot and Li Junfeng, "Renewable Energy Policy Update for China," Renewable Energy World.com, July 21, 2010.

5. China clean Energy Network, "China Clean Energy Report," December 14, 2010.

6. "Can Business Leaders Create Clean Jobs?" *Fortune*, December 6, 2010.

7. James P. Rubin, "Farewell to the Age of the Treaty," *New York Times* as reported by the *International Herald Tribune*, November 21, 2010.

8. World Challenge is a global annual competition aimed at finding projects or small businesses that have shown enterprise and innovation at grassroots levels. It is run by the BBC and *Newsweek* in association with Shell.

9. A. K. Streeter, "Powering Past Paris, Hangzhou Will Have 50,000 Bike-Share Bikes," *Treehugger,* Business and Political News, July 26, 2009.

Chapter 10

1. Hu Yuanyuan, "Premier Sets 7% Growth Target," *China Daily,* February 28, 2011.

2. Minnie Chan, "We Don't Want to Replace U.S., Says Dai Bingguo," *South China Morning Post,* December 8, 2010.

3. "Chinese President Hu Jintao's New Year Address," Xinhua News Agency, December 31, 2009.

4. "President Hu delivers New Year Address," *China Daily,* December 31, 2010.

5. Froma Harrop, "Season Brings Reminder of U.S. Reliance on China," *Honolulu Star—Advertiser,* December 21, 2010.

6. Jesse Lee, White House Blog post, January 19, 2011. See www.whitehouse.gov/blog/2011/01/19/president-obama-welcomes-president-hu-china-white-house; access date: May 10, 2011.

7. Zbigniew Brzezinski, "Redefining the U.S.-PRC Relationship," *New York Times,* January 5, 2011.

8. Henry A. Kissinger, "The U.S. and China Don't Need a Cold War," *International Herald Tribune,* January 15–16, 2011.

Afterword

1. Mike Mullen, "A Step Toward Trust with China," *International Herald Tribune,* July 25, 2011. http://www.nytimes.com/2011/07/26/opinion/26Mullen.html?_r=1

INDEX

A

ABB, 124
Afghanistan, 2, 105
Agence France-Presse, 112
Airbus, 120, 152
Air China, 120, 121
Aksai Chin, 39
Alcatel, 82
Alibaba, 52
Alibaba Group, 126, 127
Alipay, 126
Alliance Française, 109
Amazon.com, 126
American Energy Innovation
  Council, 141
Amoy Canning Corporation, 6
Amway, 82
Anderson, Eric, 40
Angola, 106, 107
Anhui Province, 79
AOL Inc., 126
Apple iPhone, 65
Areva T&D, 124
Armani, 29
ASEAN (Association of Southeast
  Asian Nations), 32, 41, 49, 80
Asian Development Bank
  Institute, 65, 66
Asia Society, 19, 31
Assembled in China, 62, 65, 68
Associated Press, 112, 133
Astroenergy Co. Ltd., 140

ATRA, 125, 126
Auctiva, 52
Augustine, Norm, 142
Australia, 134, 135, 136
Avon, 82

B

Babylon, 104
Bading Yingli, 138
Ban, Ki-moon, 105
Bangladesh, 89
Bank of America, 50, 141
Bank of China, 28, 44, 46, 50
Bank of New York Mellon, 58
Barnes, Lilace Reid, 7
Bata, 71
Bayer, 82
BBC, 113, 114, 143, 155
Beibu Gulf Economic Zone, 80
Beihai, 80
Beijing, 1, 6, 7, 10, 12, 25, 31, 33,
  34, 35, 38, 39, 40, 42, 43, 48, 49,
  50, 51, 55, 69, 70, 72, 75, 76, 77,
  81, 83, 91, 100, 101, 102, 106,
  107, 109, 110, 113, 116, 117,
  118, 121, 122, 123, 130, 135,
  139, 146, 149, 153, 155, 161
Beijing Olympics, 103
Belgium, 2
Bell Helicopter, 2
Big Mac, 101
Bisignani, Giovanni, 121

Blackstone, 50, 52
Blue Prince, 2
Blue Ribbon Sports, 8
BNP, 82
Boeing Co., 34, 44, 120, 152
Bombardier Inc., 82, 120, 122
Bongiorni, Sara, 62
Boston Consulting Group, 77, 78, 127
Bowerman, Bill, 8
Bo'ao Forum, 99
BP Amoco, 84
Branson, 101
Brazil, 109, 120, 162
Bright Food, 52
British Council, 109
Broadcom Corp., 66
Brookings Institute, 114
Brunei, 32, 39
Brzezinski, Zbigniew, 155, 156
Buckley, Chris, 188
Buddhism, 104
Buenos Aires, 133
Bulgari, 29
Burger King, 152
Burmese, 73
Burns, Ursula, 141
BYD, 72, 123

C
Cadbury PLC, 52
Cambodia, 179
Cambridge University, 110
Canada, 52, 72, 82, 109, 120, 133, 135, 136, 162
Cape Horn, 133
Casas-Zamora, Kevin, 114
Cathay Pacific, 121
CCTV, 113
Cervantes Institute, 109
Cessna, 2

Chan, Bonnie, 102
Chan, Margaret, 105
Chang, Leslie T., 70
Chang'e—2 satellite, 1
Chateauroux, 44
Chen, Joan, 101
Chengdu, 77, 79
Chery, 72
Chesapeake Energy Corp., 51
Chiang Kai-shek, 39
Chicago, 7, 37, 114, 165
Chile, 105, 133
China's Politburo, 20, 21, 23, 25
China Bistro, 152
China CITIC Bank, 58
China Construction Bank, 25, 58, 95
China Daily, 2, 6, 43, 106, 111, 113
China Development Bank Leasing Co., 120, 138
China Eastern Airline, 120
China Global Investment Tracker, 108
China Heaven Creation International Performing Arts Co., 101
China Merchants Bank, 58
China National Railway Locomotive and Rolling Stock, 82
China National Tourism Administration, 112
China Petrochemical Corp., 49
China Philharmonic Orchestra, 103
China Southern Airline, 120
China–United States Exchange Foundation, 36
Chinese Ministry of Education, 110
Chongqing, 25, 72, 77, 79, 81

Chongzuo, 80
CIC (China Investment Corp.), 50
Citigroup, 50, 58
Citroen, 84
Claremont McKenna College, 111
Clavell, James, 9
Climate Institute (Australia), 137
Clinton, Hillary, 32, 36–37
CNN, 2, 27, 101, 113, 155
CNOOC, 51, 139
Coca Cola, 34, 50, 82, 84, 125
Coda Holdings, 153
Coddington, Grace, 102
Columbia Pictures, 91
Commercial Aircraft Corporation
  of China Ltd (COMAC), 120
Communist Party, 10, 20, 22, 23,
  38, 64, 90, 95, 112, 127
Confucius, 27, 109
Congo, 106, 107
ConocoPhilips, 52
Cooper, Gary, 17
Cooper, Helene, 42
CPPCC (Chinese People's Political
  Consultative Conference),
  36, 163
CRI (China Radio
  International), 113
Crouching Tiger, Hidden
  Dragon, 101
Cruise, Tom, 35

D
Dai, Bingguo, 148
Dalai Lama, 39, 95–96
Dalian, 77
Danone, 75
Dell, 69, 75
Deng Xiaoping, 10, 12, 18, 21,
  24, 26, 64, 151, 153, 155
Dentyne, 8

de Rothschild, Sir Evelyn, 9
de Soysa, Indra, 42
Detert, Neal, 189
Diaoyu Islands, 39, 48, 150
Doerr, John, 142
Dolce and Gabbana, 103
Dongfang Electric Corp., 138
Dongfeng Motors, 72, 84
Dong Tao, 63
Dongting Lake, 83
Du Juan, 102
DuPont, 83, 141

E
East-West Center, 11
eBay, 52, 126
Egypt, 42, 104, 110, 160
Eisenhower, President Dwight, 12
Embraer, 120
Ericsson AB, 82, 83, 117
Esprit Holdings Ltd., 11
EU (European Union), 44, 49,
  116, 121, 122
Exploratorium, 91

F
Facebook Inc, 126, 128
Factory Girls, 70
Fangchenggang, 80
Farewell My Concubine, 101
FAW Group Corporation, 72
Fiorucci, Elio, 103
Forbe's list, 1
Ford, President, Gerald, 156
Ford Motors, 83
Foreign Affairs journal, 50
Fortune magazine, 10, 76, 77
Four Seasons Hotels, 29
Foxconn Technology, 69
France, 44, 52, 72, 74, 120,
  125, 162

Fravel, M. Taylor, 40
Fu Chengyu, 139
Fudan University, 100
Fujian Province, 24, 76, 80
Fujitsu, 84
Fuzhou, 76

G
G20, 12, 44, 162
G8, 12, 162
Gao Xingjian, 101
Gates, Bill, 141, 146
Gates, Robert, 33
Geely, 72, 73
Geithner, Tim, 58, 94, 95
General Electric, 34, 81, 82, 120,
    138, 141, 152
Germany, 37, 38, 49, 68, 72, 74,
    136, 138, 162
Gibbs, Bob, 47
GI Bill, 17
Giddens, Lord Anthony, 134, 135
Global China Connection
    (GCC), 111
GM (General Motors), 84,
    142, 152
Goethe Institute, 109
Goldwind Science and Technology
    Co., 138
Google Inc., 127, 128, 141
GPS Systems, 63
Grameen Bank, 89
Gramophone Magazine, 103
Great Wall, 14, 104
Greece, 49
Greenpeace, 138
Guangdong, 25, 64, 74, 81, 82,
    83, 118, 161
Guangxi Zhuang autonomous
    region, 80
Guangzhou, 1, 74, 77, 79, 83

Guardian Newspaper, 44, 110
Gucci, 29
Gulangyu, 5, 6
Gunsmoke, 61

H
Hafei, 72
Haier, 82
Hainan Airline, 120
Hainan Island, 25, 36, 80
Hale, David D., 50
Hale, Lyric Hughes, 50
Han, 73
Hangzhou Bicycle Rental Co., 144
Harbin Engineering
    University, 115
Harrop, Froma, 151
Henan Province, 81
Heritage Foundation, 108
Hero, 101
Hewlett-Packard, 69, 79
HKUST (Hong Kong University
    of Science and Technology),
    11, 109
Hoechst, 83
Holliday, Chad, 141
Hollywood, 14, 35, 101, 102
Honda, 69
Honeywell International, 34
Hong Kong, 1, 2–3, 5, 6, 7–11,
    15, 29, 31, 36, 38, 49, 50, 51,
    54, 63, 64, 68, 79, 80, 82, 90,
    91, 92, 93, 94, 99, 109, 110,
    111, 118, 120, 122, 128, 138,
    149, 161
Hong Kong General Chamber of
    Commerce, 9, 10
Hong Kong Stock Exchange, 2,
    11, 26, 52
Hong Kong–Taipei Business
    Cooperative Committee, 9

Hong Kong's Polytechnic Fashion School, 103
Hon Hai Precision Industry Co., 69
Hormats, Robert, 6
HSBC, 82
Hu, President Jintao, 21, 31, 33, 43, 44, 98, 125, 136, 148, 149, 153, 155, 163, 165, 172, 177
Hua Ercheng, 95
Huaneng Power, 82
Huangyan Island, 39
Huawei Technologies Co. Ltd., 34, 117
Huayi Group, 102
Hubei Province, 81, 84
Huffington Post, 188
Humboldt squid, 133
Husk Power Systems (India), 144
Hussein, Saddam, 34
HXMT (Hard X-ray Modulation Telescope), 124
Hyundai, 74, 82

I
IATA, 121
IBM, 8, 115, 116
ICBC, 58
Idei, Nobuyuki, 91
IFF (International Flavors and Fragrances Inc.), 75
I Love Lucy, 61
IMF (International Monetary Fund), 32, 53, 104, 162, 175
Immelt, Jeff, 141
Inchcape Pacific Ltd., 9, 90, 91
India, 38, 39, 54, 68, 102, 104, 118, 144, 162
Indonesia, 32, 36, 54, 118, 135
Infineon Tecnologies AG, 66
Ingersoll, 83
Intel Corporation, 66, 79, 116

International Finance Corp., 108
Iraq, 2, 34, 37, 105
Italy, 72, 162

J
Jaguar Computer, 116
Jiang, President Jemin, 10, 21
Jiangsu Province, 25, 69, 76, 140
Jiangxi Province, 137
Jiao Tong University, 125
JingAO Solar Co. Ltd., 138
Johnson, Senator Lyndon B., 11
Jones, Gary, 102

K
Kansas City, 74
KaraKoram Highway, 106
Keating, Admiral Timothy, 35
Kellog School, 109
Kelly, John, 116
Kennedy, President John F., 12, 17, 62
KFC (Kentucky Fried Chicken), 75, 152
Kimberly-Clark, 83
Kim Jong-il, 151
Kissinger, Henry, 156
Kleiner Perkins Caufield & Byers, 142
Knight, Phil, 8
KOK Machinery, 69
Korea, North, 32, 35, 39, 150, 151, 154
Korea, South, 35, 39, 41, 55, 66, 68, 99, 130, 133, 134, 150
Kraft Foods, 52, 75
Kyoto Protocol, 142

L
Ladd, Alan, 17
Lady Gaga, 101

La Farge, 82
Lake Forest College, 7
Lam, Kam Chuen, 13
Lao, Zi, 98, 140
Laos, 80
Laotian, 73
Lardy, Nicholas, 95
LDK Solar Co. Ltd., 137–138
Lee, Kuan Yew, 99
Lee, President Myung-bak, 35
Leider, Richard, 10
Lesotho National Library, 106
Levin, Richard, 110
Levitt, William, 61
Levittown, 61
Li, Changchun, 112
Li, Keqiang, 21, 49, 163
Li, Peng, 10
Lin, Justin, 105
Link (REIT) Management Ltd., 11
Listerine, 8
Liu, Jianchao, 99
Liu Wen, 102
Lloyds of London, 58
Lockheed Martin Corporation, 34
London School of Economics, 134
Long Term Evolution (LTE)
    network, 117
Lu, Ping, 10
Lui, Yvonne, 111
LVMH, 29

M
Macao, 10, 49, 79, 82, 122
"Made in America," 62, 68
"Made in China," 14, 62, 63, 101
"Made in Indonesia," 62
"Made in Philippines," 62
"Made in Sri Lanka," 62
"Made in U.S.A.," 62
"Made in Vietnam," 62

Malaysia, 8, 32
Manchu Wok, 152
Manulife-Sinochem, 76
Mao, Zedong, 3, 38
Maplecroft.NET Ltd., 136
Mastercard Inc., 46
McDonald's, 75, 81, 152
McDonnell Douglas, 120
McKinsey & Co., 74, 77
Mearsheimer, John, 37
Meisel, Steve, 102
Mencius, 98
Mickey Mouse, 101
Microsoft Corp., 101, 117, 126
Midford, Paul, 42
Milan Fashion Week, 103
Millennium Development Goals,
    105, 106, 175
Ming Dynasty, 104
Minneapolis, 61
Minute Maid, 125
MIT, 40
Mitsubishi, 81, 83, 84, 138
Morgan Stanley, 50, 54, 58,
    68, 102
Motorola, 82, 83
Moyo, Dambisa, 108
Murray, Senator Patty, 67
Myanmar, 80, 106, 154
MySpace Inc., 126

N
Nanjing, 24, 38, 82–83, 90,
    91, 92
Nanning, 80, 122
Nansha Archipelago, 39
National Ballet of China, 103
National Peking Opera Co., 103
National People's Congress,
    20, 21, 22, 147, 159,
    160, 169

National Retail Federation
(US), 67
National University of Defense
Technology, 116
NDRC (National Development
and Reform Commission),
79, 139
New York Stock Exchange, 51, 138
New York Times, 42, 142, 155
Ningbo, 76, 77, 84
Nissan, 70, 72
Nixon, President Richard, 19, 29,
62, 156
N. M. Rothschild & Sons, 9
Nokia, 81, 82, 83
Norfolk, 41
Nvidia Corporation, 116
Nye, Joseph, 97, 112, 114, 165

O
Oak Ridge National Laboratory,
116
Obama, Michelle, 102
Obama, President Barack, 19, 36,
40, 43, 44, 67, 94, 101, 102,
111, 153, 161, 165, 172
OECD, 118
OEM (Original equipment
manufacturer), 64
OOCL (Orient Overseas
Container Line), 36
Opium War, 99
Owens, Admiral Bill, 36
Oxford University, 110

P
P. F Chang's, 152
PAI Partners, 52
Pakistan, 106, 134
Panda Express, 152
Papua New Guinea, 133

Payack, JJ
PBDC (People's Bank of China),
28, 44, 50
Peace Hotel, 29
Pearl Harbor, 38
Pearl River Delta, 79, 80, 82, 83
Peking duck, 75
Peking University, 6
Peninsula Hotels, 29
People's Republic of China, 3, 19,
24, 27, 38, 72, 104
Pepsico, 75, 82, 83
Peterson Institute, 47, 95
Philippines, 32, 35, 39, 99, 143
Phillips, 83
Piano Island, 6
Pilkington Glass, 84
Pizza Hut, 75, 152
PLA (People's Liberation Army),
22, 23
Portugal, 44, 49
Power Corp. of Canada, 82
Preparatory committee, 10
Proctor & Gamble Co., 8, 75,
76, 82
Pudong, 29
Puxi, 29

Q
Qiao, Shi, 10
Qingdao, 76, 77, 82, 140
Qing Dynasty, 38, 104
Qinzhou, 80

R
Ralph Lauren, 101
Recovery Act (U.S.), 141
Renminbi (Yuan), 3, 43
Repsol YPF SA, 49
Reuters, 103, 112, 119
Richardson-Merrell, Inc., 8

Ritz Carlton Hotels, 29
Roach, Stephen, 54
Ruijin Hospital, 125
Russia, 18, 42, 72, 103, 122, 150, 162

S
Sachs, Jeffrey, 68
Safran Group, 120
SAIC, 72, 152
Sail (GM model), 152
Salazar, Ken, 141
Samsung Group, 66
San Diego, 40, 56
Santiago, 133
Sanyo, 84
Sarkozy, President Nicolas, 44
Schell, Orville, 19–20
Schick, 8
Schwab, Klaus, 106
SDR (Special Drawing Right), 57, 174
"Seven Days in Tibet," 91
Shandong Province, 76, 140
Shanghai, 1, 24, 26, 29, 72, 77, 79, 80, 81, 82, 99, 109, 111, 122, 125, 135, 176
Shaoshan, 83
Shaoshan village, 83
Shapiro, David, 10
Sharp, 83
Shenzhen, 24, 64, 69, 70, 74, 77, 79, 82, 118, 123
Sichuan Province, 72, 75, 79, 82
Siemens, 82, 83, 84, 122, 124, 125, 138
Singapore, 8, 9, 83, 99
Sino-Congolese Friendship Hospital, 106
Sinopec, 52
Sinovel Wind Co. Ltd., 138

Smithsonia National Museum of History, 102–103
SOE (State-owned enterprise), 25, 119
Soft Power, 12, 97–114
Solso, Tim, 141
Sony, 69, 91, 92
South Africa, 106, 107, 135, 143, 176
South China Morning Post, 19, 102, 116, 125, 133, 148
Southdale Center, 61
Southeast Asia Nuclear Weapons-Free Zone, 41
South Tibet, 39
Soviet Union, 12, 32, 38, 105, 155
Space, Zack, 47
Spain, 49
Spencer Stuart & Associates, 9
Sprint Nextel, 34
Sri Lanka, 62
Standard Chartered, 82
Stephens, Bret Louis, 131
Stiglitz, Joseph, 57
STMicroelectronics NV, 66
Stockholm International Peace Research Institute, 42
Sudan, 42, 154, 171
Sui, Anna, 102
Sunlight Foundation, 35
Suntech, 138
Suyan Rock, 39
Suzhou, 76, 77, 83, 140
Swaine, Michael, 40

T
Taiping Rebellion, 38
Taiwan (ROC), 6, 32, 39, 41, 64, 69, 80, 84, 95, 103, 110, 129, 130, 167
Taizhou, 76

Tam, Vivienne, 102, 103
Tanzania, 106, 108
Taoism, 104
Tau Kappa Epsilon, 7
Tazara Railway, 106
Teck Resources, 50
Tencent Holdings, 126
The Civil War, 38
The Great Wall, 14, 104
The Guardian, 44, 110
Three Gorges Dam, 84, 138
3Leaf Systems, 34
Tianhe-1A, 116
Tianjin, 7, 38, 72, 77, 81, 83, 99, 100, 116, 122
Tibet Autonomous Region, 51, 80
Times Square, NYC, 113, 114
Tokyo, 9, 35
Top Gun (movie), 35
Toray Engineering, 81
Toshiba Corp., 66
Toyota, 70, 72, 83, 84
Treaty of Amity and Cooperation, 41
Treaty of Nanking, 6
Treaty of Tianjin, 38
Trident, 8
Tsingtao beer, 82
Tung, Chee-Hwa, 36
Twitter Inc., 126, 128, 130
2Wire Inc., 34
Tyler, Tony, 121

U
UN (United Nations), 104, 105
UNESCO (United Nations Education, Science and Cultural Organization), 103, 104
Unilever, 83, 84
United Press International, 112
University of California, 56, 73
University of Hawaii, 7
University of Oregon, 8
University of Pennsylvania, 8, 56
UN Security Council, 32, 105, 170, 171
Upjohn, 83
U.S. Bancorp, 58
U.S. Chamber of Commerce, 9, 10, 35
U.S. China Business Council, 155
U.S. Congress, 19, 34, 52, 54, 142, 165
U.S. National Retail Federation, 67
USNS *Comfort*, 105
USNS *Mercy*, 105
USS *George Washington*, 35
Uygur, 80

V
Vendio, 52
Venezuela, 109
Vick Chemical, 8
Vietnam, 32, 39, 54, 80, 118
Vivid Economics Report, 137
Vogue magazine, 102
Volkswagen, 72

W
Wang, Feng, 73
Wang, Guoqing, 100
Wang, Vera, 102
Wang, Zhenyi, 125
Wanjiang River Urban Belt, 79
Warner Lambert Co., 8
Washington, DC, 35, 66, 95, 137, 169, 173
Wayne, John, 17
Weaver, Dallas, 131, 132
Wells Fargo, 58
Wen, Premier Jiabao, 27, 100, 110, 146, 163

Wharton, 8, 56, 93, 115
WikiLeaks, 150
Willard, Admiral Robert, 35, 36
Wilson, Sir David, 9
Wintour, Anna, 102
World Bank, 32, 53, 57, 104, 105, 108
World Economic Forum, 100, 106
World War II, 7, 17, 37, 38
WTO (World Trade Organization), 12, 32, 66, 104, 143, 173
Wu, Jason, 102, 103
Wuhan, 77, 84
Wuhu, 80
Wuxi, 83

X
Xi, Jinping, 6, 21, 22, 24, 25, 163, 169
Xia, Faye, 75
Xiamen, 5, 6, 24
Xiaolangdi dam, 81
Xing, Yuqing, 189
Xinhua News Agency, 113
Xinjiang Autonomous Region, 51, 80
Xinyu town, 137, 138
Xisha Archipelago, 39
Xi Zhongxun, 24

Y
Yahoo Inc., 126
Yale University, 68, 110

Yalu River, 39
Yan, Alice, 191
Yang, Admiral Yi, 39
Yang, Jiechi, 95
Yangtze River Delta, 79, 80, 82, 83
Yao, Ming, 101
Yellow Sea, 35, 36, 134
Yenching University, 6
Yeoh, Michelle, 101
Yi, Gang, 44
Yin Ruins, 104
YMCA, 7
YouTube LLC, 126, 128
Yuan, 3, 4, 28, 47, 48, 49, 50, 53, 58, 67, 88, 157
Yulin, 80
Yum! Brands, 181
Yum! Group, 75
Yunus, Muhammad, 89
YWCA, 7

Z
Zakaria, Fareed, 27
Zambia, 106, 107
Zh ng, Ziyí, 101
Zhejiang Province, 24, 76, 81, 84, 140, 144
Zheng, Bijian, 99
Zhi, Lily, 102
Zhongshan Automotive, 72
Zhou, Xiaochuan, 57
Zhu, Rongji, 10
Zhu, Weiqun, 95
Zimbabwe, 42